MW01122211

Aesthetic Violence
and Women in Film

Aesthetic Violence and Women in Film is a highly readable and timely analysis of the intersection of two recent cinematic trends in martial arts films: aesthetic violence and warrior women.

Joseph Kupfer establishes specific categories of aesthetic film violence, including hyper-violence, a visual style that emphasizes the sensuous surface of physical destruction and surreal violence, when spectacular imagery and gravity-defying dance replace blood and gore. He then goes on to outline the ascendancy during the past decades of female characters to the status of hero in action films. Interweaving these two subjects, the book reveals how women warriors instigate and animate the models of aesthetic violence introduced. The hyper-violence of *Kill Bill* celebrates the triumphs of the Bride, whose maiming and dismemberment of enemies produce brilliant red plumes and silvered geysers of blood. The surrealistic violence in *Crouching Tiger, Hidden Dragon* and *The House of Flying Daggers* creatively elevates violence from earthbound mayhem to an enchanting aerial display of female-dominated acrobatics. Both film-stories are driven by the plight and aspirations of female combatants, suggesting an affinity between women and the transfiguration of fighting wrought by surrealistic violence.

By elevating the significance of violence in action films and linking it together with the growing popularity of central female characters in this genre, *Aesthetic Violence and Women in Film* will be of interest to students and scholars in film studies, popular culture, gender studies, aesthetics, and social philosophy.

Joseph H. Kupfer is University Professor Philosophy at Iowa State University, USA, where he teaches ethics, aesthetics, and medical ethics. Recent articles deal with virtue, sainthood, and philosophy in film. His previous book was *Meta-Narrative in the Movies: Tell Me a Story* (2014).

Aesthetic Violence and Women in Film

Kill Bill with *Flying Daggers*

Joseph H. Kupfer

Routledge
Taylor & Francis Group

LONDON AND NEW YORK

First published 2018
by Routledge
2 Park Square, Milton Park, Abingdon, Oxon OX14 4RN

and by Routledge
711 Third Avenue, New York, NY 10017

Routledge is an imprint of the Taylor & Francis Group, an informa business

British Library Cataloguing-in-Publication Data
A catalogue record for this book is available from the British Library

Library of Congress Cataloging-in-Publication Data
Names: Kupfer, Joseph H. author.
Title: Aesthetic violence and women in film : Kill Bill with flying daggers /
    Joseph H. Kupfer.
Description: London ; New York : Routledge, 2018. | Includes index.
Identifiers: LCCN 2017059597 | ISBN 9780415785518 (hardback :
    alk. paper) | ISBN 9781315228143 (ebook)
Subjects: LCSH: Violence in motion pictures. | Women heroes in motion
    pictures.
Classification: LCC PN1995.9.V5 K87 2018 | DDC 791.43/655—dc23
LC record available at https://lccn.loc.gov/2017059597

ISBN: 978-0-415-78551-8 (hbk)
ISBN: 978-1-315-22814-3 (ebk)

Typeset in Times New Roman
by Apex CoVantage, LLC

For Gabi, a true woman warrior

Contents

Acknowledgements

I am grateful to Iowa State University for a sabbatical during which much of the book was written.

Introduction

Bonnie and Clyde: ending as beginning

Recall the stunning climax of Arthur Penn's award-winning film *Bonnie and Clyde* (1967). After a winding diet of robbery, murder and frenzied vehicular get-aways, the outlaws meet their bloody end. The young, attractive criminals are riddled with bullets whose impact buffets them about like rag dolls. The bandits gaze knowingly at one another just before their execution. It is announced with a flourish when a flock of birds takes flight, as if fleeing the impending destruction, with a powerful beating of their wings. The moment of death is extended in slow-motion as the deafening noise of machine gun and rifle fire drowns out the flapping of the birds. Prolonging the death scene crystallizes their union, cinematically immortalizing their mortality.

The death scene does several other things that work in different, sometimes opposite, directions. It creates an air of unreality because enough bullets are fired to wipe out a battalion of soldiers, bouncing the bodies of the couple in a protracted spectacle of annihilation. People do not look like this in real life when shot. Yet the drawn-out carnage and explosion of gunfire also make it all too real, reinforcing the overwhelming impact of the attack. The urge of the lawmen to overkill makes narrative sense as the criminals have wreaked havoc on banks, citizens and police. The relentless fusillade also fits within the arc of the story. As it progresses, the escapes of the robbers get narrower and the damage they sustain more severe.

Nevertheless, the death of Bonnie and Clyde is elevated to a special event. Not only is their capture commemorated, but so is their brief fling on the public stage. Indeed, it becomes apparent (either during the viewing or in its subsequent interpretation) that the death is itself staged – as a planned event within the narrative as well as a cinemagraphic moment. As narrative incident, the ambush is staged by the law enforcement officers in league with the father of the duo's goofy young sidekick. As artistic creation, the finale is orchestrated through cinematic manipulation and the implacable arc of retribution. The image of the outlaws jerking about like hapless marionettes suggests that they lacked genuine control of their lives. Perhaps they were mere puppets all along.

Penn's dramatic ending seems to straddle two poles of movie mayhem. The first is the more or less realistic treatment of violence in the movies in which the audience is invited to the time-honored "suspension of disbelief." We watch as if viewing real cowboys, soldiers, or criminals engage in wounding, maiming and killing their enemies. Such realistic or quasi-realistic violence ("realistic" from now on) continues today as a staple of movie violence in genres ranging from science fiction and film noir, to drama and romantic adventure. In such films, the violence propels the plot or is the outcome of narrative events and the characters that move them.

Yet more recently, movies have taken a different approach to violence. They have transformed the violence by virtue of cinematic technique into something that could not be mistaken for the real thing. Film has aestheticized violence, providing images that are to be appreciated for the way they look, aside from their place in the story. Although movies always stylized what we saw, we were able to maintain the entertaining fiction that we were watching realistic events; shooting, stabbing, bombing could look something like this. The climactic execution of Bonnie and Clyde seems to be ambiguous. Bodies might very well react this way to interminable gunshots, yet viewers are nevertheless stunned by the sustained, relentless devastation. As indicated, the frightful amount of shooting fits nicely with the escalating violence as the story progresses, yet it seems unrealistic in its staged, slow-motion extravagance.

The ending also captures Bonnie's indispensable role as Clyde's partner in derring-do. She has been integral to the energy and depth of the story as well as to Clyde's ephemeral success. By situating Bonnie as a counterpoint to Clyde in the composition of the film's mesmerizing climax, argues Marsha Kinder, Penn can be retrospectively seen as inaugurating a new mode of action film. Categorizing the finale as "mythic," she writes, "Although *Bonnie and Clyde* combines familiar elements of the gangster genre and musical, this mythic ending helped it spawn a new subgenre of violent road movies featuring a heterosexual couple in search of justice, thrills, or fame" (2001: 72).

More recent is the emphasis on images of violence independent of or parallel to the narrative demands of film-story. The cinematic rendering of the action makes the audience aware that it is enjoying film artifice – for its own sake. Shortly after *Bonnie and Clyde*, in fact, Sam Peckinpah's depiction of violence in such films as *The Wild Bunch* (1969) could also be appreciated independent of its role in the film-story. Often using slow-motion and montage cutting, Peckinpah's films offer "striking scenes and images presented formalistically so that they are detachable from the immediate narrative context" (Prince 1999: 169). To be sure, the look of violence can contribute to or detract from the dramatic thrust of the story, as indicated with regard to *Bonnie and Clyde*. However, the aestheticization scrutinized in this book is such that riveting images are foregrounded, demanding attention in their own right. In many cases, the aestheticized violence supersedes the story which may not have been all that substantive in the first place.

What is especially salient in *Bonnie and Clyde* for my purposes is the way it privileges two powerful cinematic movements: aesthetic violence and fighting women. Rather than provide an exhaustive catalogue or sweeping topography of either aestheticized violence or warrior women in film, I offer an analysis, however partial, of the intersection or confluence of these two cinematic subjects. Doing so yields a cluster of interesting dimensions of film, some more attuned to the aesthetic aspect of violence, some more focused on gendered violence and some a robust synthesis of the two.

The violence that is examined in the following chapters is interpersonal, delivered by people doing combat with one another, rather than the more impersonal violence wrought by vehicles, firearms, incendiary devices, or natural forces. In particular, I concentrate most on films in which martial arts predominate. It is may be helpful, then, to include here a brief lexicon of the terms used to characterize the violence and their representations in Asian cinema and films influenced by it. According to L.S. Kim, "Kung fu is a term used mainly in the west; Chinese call the genre wu dar (unarmed martial arts) or wuxia (armed, mostly with swords)" (2006). The most frequently used term seems to be *wuxia*, which incorporates an element of chivalry or honor, as it is a compound of *wu* and *xia:* military or armed and honorable or heroic (Teo 2000). Although *wuxia* typically includes swordplay, *wuxia pian* more explicitly denotes martial arts combined with swordsmanship (Ching-kiu 2005: 66). More general still is *wugong* (martial skills) referring to "both hand-to-hand combat kung fu and the fighting skills of using weapons" (Li 2005: 51). *Wugong* is more general then *wuxia pian* because weaponry can go beyond swords to include arrows, spears, knives and all sorts of improvised implements of the everyday. I note these terms chiefly for the sake of fidelity to the discourse on martial arts films even though I tend to stick to the more familiar *wuxia*.

Aestheticized violence

The aestheticization that shapes my cinematic analyses tends to be the product of photographic and editing artifice. By means of such technological ingenuity as digitization, movies have elaborated on a tradition of Asian film-making that dates back to the 1920s which includes a fantasy component, what Stephen Teo cites as *shenguai wuxia:* sword and sorcery or sword and magic (2005: 192). The two films that I discuss as paradigms of the fullest aesthetic treatment of violence, *Crouching Tiger, Hidden Dragon* (Ang Lee, 2000) and *House of Flying Daggers* (Zhang Yimou, 2004), certainly celebrate this fantastic dimension of *wuxia* or *wugong.* Acrobatic hand-to-hand and weaponized fighting in these films all but eliminate the blood and dismemberment that characterize other modes of aesthetically rendered cinematic violence.

Culminating in a characterization of this fantastic portrayal of *wuxia* fighting, the first chapter provides my own taxonomy of aesthetic violence in film. I begin with the minimally aesthetic value of excessive mayhem, categorizing it as "mega-violence." The term "mega- violence" signifies great quantities or accumulations of violence. Scenes of violence that are extreme are not especially noteworthy for their aesthetic features. For that reason mega-violence is minimally aesthetic. Great quantity of blood-letting, bodily destruction or killing does not in itself yield images rich in aesthetic qualities. The mega-violence that typifies so many Schwarzenegger films, for example, consists of large amounts violence piled on top of a glut of preceding violence. Yet quantitative enlargement is not by itself a qualitative transformation of the violence that is depicted.

Repetition can, however, create an aesthetically charged experience. Think here of an evening sky crammed with stars or thousands of migrating birds alighting in one area, such as the sand hill cranes in Iowa. Monumental volumes of violence can make an artful impact, as layering enormous human destruction into a crisp sequence of scenes can be exhilarating. A cavalcade of injury, blood and annihilation can produce the almost visceral aesthetic of power, as in the overwhelming force witnessed in such natural disasters as hurricanes or volcanoes.

Mega-violence is especially aesthetic, moreover, when the destructive forces are structured rhythmically, over several scenes. By punctuating extremely violent episodes with periods of relative calm, films can weld the mega-violence into a larger pattern. One very effective pattern is building the violence to a crescendo. Instead of violence that dims or merely repeats, violence that escalates over an extended stretch of time imparts an aesthetic of kinesthetic and dramatic ascent. Rhythmically arranged violence can thereby infuse mega-violence with an aesthetic dimension lacking or greatly reduced in cinematic violence that is simply over the top. Because of such considerations, I understand extreme or excessive violence as occupying an aesthetic place adjacent to more artful forms of cinematic violence: hyper- and surrealistic violence.

Hyper-violence is one of two modes of cinematic fighting in which the violence is actually transformed in an aesthetically attractive fashion. Hyper-violence does so by lavishing camera and editing technology on the sensuous surface of physical destruction. For example, the slow-motion severing of an arm or the eruption of pulsing blood can only be produced by means of inventive camera-work or film-editing. The violence can be considered "hyper" because it is above and beyond the simple excesses of realistic representations (including those found in mega-violence); it is hyperbolic in exaggerating images of the bodily damage wrought by such weapons as swords, knives and pikes. Hyper-violence intensifies the effects of bodily onslaught, for example, by enlarging the spatter of blood or vivifying its pattern. The results are alluring, painterly images set in motion by individuals doing battle to the death.

Unlike hyper-violence, the second mode of artfully transfigured violence eschews blood and gore, replacing the grisly destruction of mega- and hyper-violence with the graceful movement of cinematically creative choreography. The hallmarks of violence that is surrealistically portrayed are beauty and gravity-defying dance instead of harsh fisticuffs, bloody wounding and lethal destruction. In surrealistically staged violence, the actions of the characters defy the laws of gravity as well as the limits of the human body. Slow-motion tracking shots of arrows and knives consort with the digitization that yields characters vaulting over rooftops and scampering up walls or simply soaring through space. The violent action is transformed by the filmmaker into elaborate aerial acrobatics. The fact that so much of the combat includes airborne bodily maneuvering, free of earth's inexorable pull, suggests symbolic meaning in the liberation from the norms that restrict conventional social life. The liberation, moreover, belongs to women.

Women warriors

This is the second subject of the book, interwoven with aestheticized violence: the ascendancy of female characters to the status of hero in action films. No longer an auxiliary or sidekick of a male protagonist, women are increasingly taking over the lead role in films of interpersonal violence. The character of Bonnie represents a plausible place to locate the beginning of a major shift in the portrayal of women in action films. A cold-blooded, female outlaw who enjoys the chase, gunplay and killing points the way to yet more full-blooded women warriors. Chapter 2 provides an overview of the evolution of the female lead of action film: moving from someone like Bonnie whose violent behavior depends on Clyde as both his girl and gunsel moll to women who break free of such narrative limitations. Among transition action women are Thelma and Louise (*Thelma and*

Louise, Ridley Scott, 1991), whose journey into violence is not deliberate but is thrust upon them. The duo also possesses another pivotal feature of the valiant woman: she only lashes out in self-defense, thereby occupying the moral high ground with regard to blood-letting and killing. Thelma and Louise, moreover, are responding to male aggression and callousness and must shed the trappings of conventional womanhood in order to liberate themselves from the role of victims.

Later female warriors will be more fully independent of men; all on their own, they will vanquish their enemies with fists and weapons. For many films, however, women protagonists seem to do little more than replace their male forerunners: they are muscular and brutal. Such characters as Angelina Jolie as Lara Croft (*Lara Croft: Tomb Raider:*Simon West, 2001) and Linda Hamilton as Sarah Connor (*Terminator:*James Cameron, 1984) seem to follow closely in the footsteps of the characters inhabited by the likes of Arnold Schwarzenegger and Jean Claude Van Damme. The heroines of our two *wuxia* films of surrealistic violence mark a striking break with the bicep-flexing, tough-guy female fighters who more densely populate the action films in which women are central.

As with their male counterparts and forerunners, female action heroes are typically unable to enjoy heterosexual romantic relationships. This limitation or obstacle may be more significant for these women than male protagonists in that women have for so long been represented as needing both protection from and involvement with men. Perhaps it is because romance does not connect easily, for filmmakers or audiences, with a woman whose nature and behavior so radically diverge from the norms that have defined women in film as much as in real life. Having liberated women from their dependence on men through the construction of the woman warrior, movies have a hard time reestablishing emotional intimacy in a novel and credible manner. The fighting prowess of female action heroes challenges typical gender norms and expectations in ways that can be disconcerting.

Self-sufficient, powerful women can seem threatening, especially to male audiences. In order to make the woman warrior more acceptable, movies address her intimidating status in various ways. One such way, for example, is to emphasize the sexual attractiveness of the character, thereby softening or containing the threat of her physical forcefulness. By exaggerating her sexuality, often through provocative attire or dialogue, the fighting female is brought into line with the more familiar norms of her gender. Her enhanced sexuality reestablishes the feminine identity of the formidable woman, giving her the aura of availability. Playing up the erotic appeal of the female star mitigates her danger by satisfying male fantasies of women; she is now brought reassuringly within the orbit of male desire. Whether eroticizing the female action hero is adequate to the demands of her disturbing persona is further explored in this chapter.

I am primarily interested in women warriors who are skilled in the martial arts that define *wuxia* film. They are the protagonists, as well as many of the supporting characters, in the three films that receive the bulk of attention in this book. Chapter 3 explores the hyper-violence that makes *Kill Bill* (Quentin Tarantino, 2003), especially *Volume I*, such an interesting and compelling film. I regard this film as a paradigm of hyper-violence, although the hyper-violent pyrotechnics only occur during the elaborate and prolonged climax of the film-story of *Volume I*. What distinguishes hyper-violence from its aesthetic neighbors in cinematic combat is the technologically manipulated visual surface of human destruction. It resembles mega-violence in that the actions of the characters are relatively realistic; they are within the capabilities of actual people. Wielding a sword or hurling a knife the way the Bride and her antagonists do could occur in the real world, outside cinema.

On the other hand, the visual effects of these actions require movie-making manipulation and could not occur in ordinary life. Hyper-violence shares its dependence on camera-work and digitization with surrealistic violence; however, the non-realistic aspects of surrealistic violence are found in the spectacular movements of the characters, not in the effects of their violent action. The destructive images of hyper-violent action, at least in the hands of Quentin Tarantino, celebrate the spurts and gouts of blood that issue from an assortment of slashes and amputations. The slow-motion lopping off of an arm or leg and the accompanying gush of blood can only be realized through the artful deployment of camera, editing or digitized image-making. The violence is aestheticized through the enhancement of the bodily destruction of one person by another. Hyper-violence magnifies the effects of physical carnage, for example, by focusing upon the spatter of blood, enriching its color, and isolating its pattern.

During the height of the Bride's battle with legions of male yakuza, Tarantino embellishes the hyper-violence by supplanting the saturated color with striking black and white. Although black and white photography is often used to reinforce a sense of bleak cinematic realism, as in film noir, in *Kill Bill* it actually contributes to the unreality of hyper-violence. The blood that squirts from a severed arm, for instance, is shown in a silver spume. When the Bride slices off an enemy's head, metallic blood shoots straight up from his mangled neck, and from another yakuza yet more mercury-tinged blood flies from his arm after its hand has been whacked off. Translating the rich red of blood briefly into the stark idiom of black and white recasts the hyper-violence in an aesthetically uncanny way, creating a change of pictorial tempo.

Although hyper-violence is primarily reserved for the Bride's triumphal marathon battle with the male yakuza, her skirmishes with various women are significant with respect to the themes that predominate in films in which female fighters carry the action and film-story. Among these themes are the challenges to gender norms that involve fighting, femininity, romantic involvement, and family. For example, over the course of the two installments of *Kill Bill*, the Bride kills three of her former female assassin colleagues (one indirectly); her battles with two other women culminate in another fatality and a standoff. Violation of the norms that typically govern femininity is magnified when women battle one another. In addition, the Bride directly destroys the domestic aspirations of her erstwhile friend Vernita when she storms her suburban home and slays her in the presence of Vernita's young daughter. This parallels the near-death experience of the Bride herself, the event that sets in motion the plot of the pair of films.

The Bride is pregnant with the child of her nefarious boss, Bill, and flees him precisely because she wants a life for her child that is different from her own – the life of an assassin. The Bride's perception of the opposition between a healthy domestic future for her offspring and the world of violence, then, fuels her ill-fated decision to seek a new life with an ordinary husband instead of rearing the child with Bill. During her wedding rehearsal (hence, the Bride), Bill and his killer cohort mow down the wedding party and leave the pregnant Bride for dead. Emerging from a years-long coma, the Bride seeks revenge on Bill and his gang and that is the engine that drives the two installments of the film-story. Only at the conclusion of the second portion do we discover, with the Bride, that her baby did not die when she was apparently mortally wounded. A lovely little girl, about the same age as Vernita's child, is living with Bill. After killing Bill, the Bride takes off with the little girl in the hopes of having the sort of motherhood that Vernita had been enjoying before the Bride careened into her California idyll. We are left to wonder whether the Bride will be able to shed her warrior skin and become a loving mother. If Bill's assessment of her is accurate, she will not succeed in beating her sword into a skillet: Bill's parting diagnosis of the Bride is that she is a "natural born killer."

Women fight, but bloodlessly and beautifully

Chapters 4 and 5 examine in depth two films that showcase surrealistic violence. Especially significant is the central role played by women in both the film-stories and the spectacle of the violence. As noted, surrealistic violence is radically removed from realistic and mega-violence in a way that hyper-violence is not. Although it shares with hyper-violence reliance on film digitization and manipulation of the movement of characters, surrealistic violence tends to elide the blood and gore found in this (and other) modes of cinematic fighting. The spilling of blood and severing of limb is replaced by fantastic bodily movement, much of which takes place off the ground.

Crouching Tiger, Hidden Dragon (Ang Lee, 2000) and *The House of Flying Daggers* (Zhang Yimou, 2004) are the two *wuxia* films that seem to me to be standard bearers of cinema that entwines surrealistic violence with the stardom of female protagonists. These emblematic Asian films creatively elevate violence from earthbound wounding and maiming to an enchanting display of aerial acrobatics and dance. Overcoming the constraints of gravity, the antagonists ricochet off buildings, run up walls, glide between rooftops and scamper among canopies of trees. Although surrealistic film violence does not (and need not) always feature women, I argue that there is an affinity between the aesthetic charm of this cinematic mode and the importance of female characters in the film-stories.

Both surrealistic films are distinctive in their focus on the plight and aspirations of women, a beautiful young woman in particular – both characters embodied by Zhang Ziyi. To be sure, the plot of *Kill Bill* also turns on the needs and interests of women, most pointedly of its hero, the Bride. Nevertheless, the narratives of our films of surrealistic violence elaborate upon gender issues in significant and sometimes poignant ways. These films raise questions concerning social roles, power and personal ambition; their surrealistic violence is woven into the fabric of the gendered conflicts. The stories of *Crouching Tiger, Hidden Dragon* and *House of Flying Daggers* are driven by women who are either precluded from the life of the martial arts or are restricted by the militarized, political institutions controlled by men. In both movies, women are ineluctably wed to violence, as the realization of their purposes and their personal growth appear to them impossible without combat – either as a necessary means to or as inherent in their long-term fulfillment.

The story of *Crouching Tiger, Hidden Dragon* is propelled by the passion of a headstrong young beauty for the life of a martial arts expert. Four people strive to win the allegiance or affection of Jen Wu (Zhang Ziyi). Renowned for their *wuxia* talents, a mature man and woman futilely try to corral Jen's zeal for combat. Li Mu Bai (Chow Yun-fat) and his would-be paramour, Yu Shu Lien (Michelle Yeoh), strive to bring the feisty young woman within the fold of accepted tradition. The first, through tutelage in the venerable lore of the martial arts, the second, through conventional marriage. Offering the alternative of life outside the traditions embodied in this reputable couple are Jen's governess, Jade Fox (Pei-pei Cheng) and a dashing young outlaw, Lo (Chang Chen). Jade has secretly been training Jen in the martial arts, herself excluded from the prestigious martial arts school of Wudan Mountain because she is a woman. As a nomadic bandit, Lo also offers a rebellious break with the norms of proper society. Jen seems torn among these various mentors or companions and the options they represent. She is certain, however, that she wants the exhilarating freedom of a woman warrior rather than the humdrum role as the wife of a nobleman with whom she is not in love.

Women are made prominent in these surrealistic action films most obviously by having them involved in all the combat, often fighting against one another. For example, the story of *Crouching Tiger, Hidden Dragon* is bookended by Jen's two protracted and inventive fights with Shu, but without the serious wounding or death found in the Bride's confrontations with women. Moreover, the most complex relationships that Jen has are with the other women, Jade Fox and Shu, not the men. In both cases, friendship is undermined by suspicion or competition. Because of their exceptional talents and yearnings, women warriors seem to have more conflicts to resolve between themselves. For example, although Jade has helped Jen become an adept in the martial arts, the girl frustrated her tutor by eclipsing the older woman.

In the singularly drawn-out, fast-paced scene in which Jen does fight men, she makes mincemeat of a throng of lumpish thugs, but performs her violence with surrealistic aplomb. Paralleling the Bride's showdown with O-Ren's yakuza, Jen's stand against a horde of male opponents also takes place inside a restaurant. Jen haughtily provokes the brawl and proceeds to spring and flip her way over, around and through her assailants. Leaving her perch on a banister, Jen glides from one railing to another, finally landing on the floor of the restaurant's second level. After executing a lithe sequence of backflips down a set of stairs, Jen scurries through the air and over the head of the man pursuing her. She follows a brisk back somersault with a lengthy upward spin that takes her back to the second story of the building. Jen deftly thrusts and parries with her sword, but draws little blood and annihilates no one. She then descends once again to the first floor of the restaurant by performing a dive with a triple-flip, as if a robed competitor in an aquatic event. After a bit of routine swordplay outside the building, Jen levitates up into the building where she freezes in a sword-brandishing posture.

Although several people die in the film-story, we never see death as the outcome of expertise in the martial arts or swordsmanship. Surrealistic violence itself is unblemished by spurts of blood, dismemberment or their fatal finale. It is as if by raising the fantastic fighting to the level of airborne dance, surrealistic violence is able to leave behind, on the ground, the bloody remains of mega- and hyper-violence.

Several aspects of *House of Flying Daggers* distinguish it from *Crouching Tiger, Hidden Dragon:* differences in story and thematic content as well as elements of its surrealism that might be considered advances over the earlier film. No longer do women battle one another; instead they form a unified front and employ their fighting skills only against men. The epony-mously named Flying Daggers is a subversive organization of women that disrupts a corrupt government and attacks its military, both of which are comprised exclusively of men. The film, then, starkly opposes women war-riors to the entrenched male regime of abusive power. The film-story also supplements the frustrated romance of *Crouching Tiger, Hidden Dragon* with the ferocious rivalry between the two men who vie for the love of the protagonist, Mei (Zhang Ziyi, again).

Unlike its predecessor, *House of Flying Daggers* incorporates clothing and weapons into its surrealistically portrayed violence. Not simply ancil-lary to the action, costuming and weaponry play essential roles in it, adding variety and novelty to the surrealistic violence. Early in the film, Mei's kimono provides a supernal transition from ballet to battle. Playing the Echo Game, Mei must duplicate the pattern created by beans tossed by the police-man (Leo) by striking numerous drums with the billowing sleeves of her kimono. She does so with an array of swirling leaps, spins and cartwheels. But the dance-like contest eventually takes a violent turn when Mei's enor-mous sleeve envelops the policeman's sword, like a prehensile tail. The swordplay that follows gives us a taste of the surrealistic fighting that will pervade the film, replete with the combatants running on air, doing impos-sible somersaults, and flipping backwards in slow-motion. The segue from enchanting dance to fantastic fighting enlivens us to the way choreography is braided together with martial arts in films in general, but especially when the violence is rendered in the surrealistic mode.

Throughout the film, surrealistic violence includes weapons, primar-ily arrows and (fittingly) daggers. For example, one of Mei's suitors, Jin, rescues the besieged woman by shooting four arrows at the quartet of her assailants. From behind, we watch the shafts magically weave their way between trees until reaching their targets. Although the arrows are (neces-sarily) released in temporal sequence, they hit the four soldiers (impossibly) at the same time. The arrows loft the attackers into the air, who proceed to pick themselves up unharmed, without losing a drop of blood.

Among the various scenes in which the trajectory of knives receives spe-cial attention is one in which they free Mei and Jin from seemingly certain doom. As the couple continues to flee the government's army (the major thread of the plot), a cascade of bamboo spears is hurled at them from the trees, trapping them in a sturdy cage. Soldiers on the ground close in, but dozens of the rebels' signature daggers hurtle into view. They plunge into the backs of the assailants, even as another wave of knives drops the remain-ing soldiers from treetops to earth. The leader of the army of green clad women unleashes a final dagger which is shown, in a trailing shot, snak-ing its way toward the enclosed couple, finally dismantling the bamboo cage. Upending the time-worn narrative of male heroes saving beleaguered women, a female phalanx now rescues a woman, saving a man in the process. Presenting airborne knives and arrows in slow-motion complements the surrealistic violence of leaping and somersaulting be-robed bodies to transform fighting into choreographed beauty purged of blood and gore – at least for the most part.

The film-story builds toward the fatal climax of the unfolding love triangle involving Mei, Jin and Leo. Several aspects of the prolonged battle between Jin and Leo at film's end are notable for their departure from every facet of violence that has preceded it. First, almost the entire fight is earthbound, devoid of the aerial allure of surrealistically orchestrated conflict. This sets the stage for the commonplace brutality that ensues; stabbing, slashing and bashing all but cripple the bloodied combatants. It is the only confrontation in the entire film-story that involves only men and it is the only fight motivated by love and jealousy. These radical violations of the movie's style and narrative put the conclusion on a different plane, isolated from the surrealistic violence that so thoroughly defines the fighting that has come before it. Instead of weakening the link between the transcendent nature of surrealistic violence and female fighters, the vicious battle between the two men who love Mei can be interpreted as bolstering it through contrast or opposition. The relationship between women and surrealistic violence emerges as a pivotal subject about which I offer a few, suggestive observations.

To recapitulate the shape of the book. Its subject is the cinematic intersection of aesthetically attractive violence with women as full-fledged action heroes. Consequently, the first two chapters develop separately and in some detail each of these foci. What then follows are analyses of three films in which women warriors instigate and animate the aestheticized violence. The hyper-violence aesthetic of *Kill Bill* contrasts with the surrealistic enchantment of *Crouching Tiger, Hidden Dragon* and *House of Flying Daggers.* Although both of these movies celebrate the martial exploits of women in fantastic, graceful movement, important differences between them repay sustained investigation.

Bibliography

Ching-kiu, Stephen Chan (2005). "The Fighting Condition in Hong Kong Cinema: Local Icons and Cultural Antidotes for the Global Popular." *Hong Kong Connections: Transnational Imagination in Action Cinema*, Eds. M. Morris, S. Li, and S. Ching-kiu, pp. 63–79. Durham, NC: Duke University Press.

Kim, L.S. (2006). "*Crouching Tiger, Hidden Dragon*: Making Women Warriors: A Transnational Reading of Asian Female Action Heroes." *Jump Cut: A Review of Contemporary Media*, 48. www.ejumpcut.org/Archive/Jc48.2006/WomenWarriors.

Kinder, Marsha (2001). "Violence American Style: The Narrative Orchestration of Violent Attractions." *Violence and American Cinema*, Ed. J. David Slocum, pp. 63–100. New York: Routledge.

Li, Leung Siu (2005). "The Myth Continues: Cinematic Kung Fu in Modernity." *Hong Kong Connections: Transnational Imagination in Action Cinema*, Eds. M. Morris, S. Leung Li, and S. Ching-kiu, pp. 49–61. Durham, NC: Duke University Press.

Prince, Stephen (1999). *Savage Cinema: Sam Peckinpah and the Rise of Ultra-Violent Movies*. Austin: University of Texas.

Teo, Stephen (2000). "Love and Swords: The Dialectics of Martial Arts Romance: A Review of *Crouching Tiger, Hidden Dragon*." http://sensesofcinema.com/2000/current-releases-11/crouching/.

——— (2005). "*Wuxia* Redux: *Crouching Tiger, Hidden Dragon* as a Model of Late Transnational Production." *Hong Kong Connections: Transnational Imagination in Action Cinema*, Eds. M. Morris, S. Leung Li, and S. Ching-kiu, pp. 191–204. Durham, NC: Duke University Press.

Filmography

Cameron, James (1984). *The Terminator*. U.S.
Lee, Ang (2000). *Crouching Tiger, Hidden Dragon*. Taiwan, U.S., H.K., Ch.
Peckinpah, Sam (1969). *The Wild Bunch*. U.S.
Penn, Arthur (1967). *Bonnie and Clyde*. U.S.
Scott, Ridley (1991). *Thelma and Louise*. U.S.
Tarantino, Quentin (2003–04). *Kill Bill (Volume I and II)*. U.S.
West, Simon (2001). *Lara Croft: Tomb Raider*. U.S.
Yimou, Zhang (2004). *The House of Flying Daggers*. H.K. and China.

1 Aestheticized violence

The book focuses on films that not only emphasize violence but manage to present it in a fashion that celebrates it by making it attractive. Despite the fact that in real life violence done by people to other individuals is usually condemned, movies manage to cast it in a positive light by rendering it in ways that are aesthetically arresting – by "aestheticizing" the violence. The term "aesthetic" or "aestheticization" is broad even when confined to cinematic violence. There is a sense in which all cinematic portrayals of violence are aesthetic insofar as they are products of film artifice: framed, shot from a particular point of view and camera angle, lighted in a distinctive way, held for a certain period of time, and located within a sequence of other shots or scenes. But let's consider such a sense of "aesthetic" as the baseline, the inescapable shaping effected by any representational art form.

Such basic aestheticization, moreover, has often been in the service of a representation that strives to be taken as more or less realistic. When watching standard fare westerns, war movies, or film noir, for example, audiences typically accept the conventions of movie-making that cue them to view the scenes *as if* actually taking place. What might be considered codes of verisimilitude. The violence enacted is taken to be approximately how violence in the real world would appear. In the past, when audiences became aware of cinematography, it was usually to signal a break with such quasi-realism: a dream, flashback, or character's viewpoint, among several movie-going conventions. But this conventional understanding has undergone some modification. Audiences are now alive to cinematic manipulations whose purpose is to shape violence in interesting and attractive ways. The sense of "aesthetic" employed here, then, is meant to indicate something more and different from the movie realism that has characterized films for decades and still epitomizes screened violence most often.

In what follows, I offer a taxonomy of cinematic violence arranged according to two aesthetic modes. One aesthetic mode involves the conceptual or structural meaning of the film; the other mode complements such meaning with the composition or form of individual movie scenes. That the interplay between the two modes should add richness and depth to movies should come as no surprise.

Aesthetic violence: conceptual and structural meaning

The types of aestheticized violence in film in the first mode flesh out the story's meaning, either conceptually or structurally. Film aesthetically frames violence for meaning in (at least) three ways: as symbolic-figurative; structurally; and as narratively essential. Because these types of aesthetic treatment of violence involve making sense of the film-story or how the narrative is organized, I think of them from the perspective of interpretive significance or cinematic meaning.

Symbolic-figurative

First, a particular shot, scene or sequence may be aesthetic because it functions symbolically or like a figure of speech. When cinematic violence is employed as a symbol, it can embody something that is related to it – directly or apposite. In the case of the film *Unforgiven* (Clint Eastwood, 1992), for instance, the ambushing of two cowboys can be interpreted as directly symbolizing the tawdriness of gun-fighting violence in the old west. Dry-gulching one cowhand in a ravine and the other in an outhouse symbolizes the way in which Western myths falsely glamorize what is rarely heroic, noble or even very dramatic. In the film, the first is portrayed as bumbling and the second as degrading; hardly the stuff of rare skill deployed courageously in the service of law and order. For another example, the comedy-drama *Junebug* (Phil Morrison, 2005) offers a sample of violence that is indirectly symbolic. When a young man, unprovoked, throws a wrench and hits his older, more favored brother, it can be viewed as symbolizing his sense of impotence at his inferior status. Years of watching his older brother praised and admired, with explicit or veiled invidious comparisons to himself, seem to crystallize in this isolated moment of film violence.

Cinematic violence can also be aesthetically nuanced by crafting analogs to literary figures of speech such as metaphor or metalepsis, metonymy or oxymoron. The violence could function as a metaphor by positioning an image to make a revealing comparison with something else. Blinding a victim could be metaphorical, for instance, for taking away a group's ability to see the truth or understand what is being done to them (say, by surreptitious oppressors). In the film *Rob Roy* (Michael Caton-Jones, 1995), a Scottish kinsman of Rob's is murdered and robbed by an Englishman. The sizable amount of money he had been transporting was to have funded

Rob's cattle-raising venture to profit the MacGregor Clan. Although Rob himself eventually evades death by the British authorities and avenges his friend's killing, the slaying of the MacGregor clansman can be viewed as a metaphor for the decline and demise of the clan system in Scotland at the hands of British hegemony during this historical period.

Alternatively, violence can serve as metalepsis, in which a part indicates a whole. Defeating an army's most distinguished general could indicate the imminence of winning the entire war. *The Fabulous Baker Boys* (Steve Kloves, 1989) includes a fairly tame moment of violence that stands in for the unacknowledged, simmering friction between the piano-playing brothers. The younger brother, Jack, flicks his brother's hand off his head when Frank persists in rearranging Jack's appearance. By the end of the film, after a more robust scene of fraternal physical conflict, we realize that the earlier hitting indicated a larger antagonism born of Jack's distaste for the lounge act the brothers have performed for fifteen years.

Classical Hollywood films avoided censorship of violence, argues Stephen Prince, by adapting the literary figure of metonymy. In metonymic displacement, an object or event stands for or takes the place of the graphic imagery of violence. Such figurative displacing of violence "adds poetic value to a scene, this poetry being located in the way that metonymy is concretized in an object or action" (2003: 221). Prince gives the example of an off-screen murder in *Scarface* (Howard Hawks, 1932) being "displaced onto the action of the falling pins" in a nearby bowling alley. The aesthetic result is that "the brutality has been sublimated poetically" (221). Although the film does not use the violence itself metonymically to displace something else, the violence is metonymically referenced.

Another use of film violence can be construed as exemplifying oxymoron or paradox, in which contradictory ideas or incompatible emotions are presented through images. I have in mind here well-known, early uses of slow-motion violence. In both *Bonnie and Clyde* (Arthur Penn, 1967) and several of Sam Peckinpah's Westerns, the excruciating violence done to the body is coupled with dance-like grace. In the climactic scene in *Bonnie and Clyde*, discussed in the Introduction, the slow-motion sequence expresses "both the spastic and the balletic" qualities of the gangsters' death (Crowdus and Porton 1993: 12). The herky-jerky spasms of the bullet-riddled pair is at odds with the leisurely and prolonged flow of their demise, producing an oxymoronic figure.

Prince offers an alternative, cognate way of expressing the paradoxical tension created by slow-motion violence. Discussing Sam Peckinpah's use of the technique in such films as *The Wild Bunch* (1969), Prince observes that the director had to keep his slow-motion shots brief in order to "accentuate the lyrical appearance of the human body acted upon by violent physical forces" (2003 : 63). For Prince, the lyrical contrasts with the violated body. The contrast is generated because the violated body is no longer under the victim's control: "slow motion is especially powerful when it correlates with a character's loss of volition" (59). The lyrical arc of the body is in tension with its powerlessness. For then, the cinematic violence also contrasts the brutality of physical violence with the graceful beauty bestowed by the filming technique.

When I investigate the aesthetic violence in our concluding pair of *wuxia* films (Chapters 4 and 5), we will see that their use of slow-motion reverses Peckinpah's approach twice over. First, the graceful effects of retarding movement noted by Prince express the volition and skill of the perpetrators of violence rather than the enervating impact of violence on its victims: slow-motion abets the active rather than the passive aspect of violence. Second, perhaps as a result of this shift in emphasis to volition, scenes of slow-motion violence are extended in space and time rather than being abbreviated. Instead of the contrast found in the paradoxical employment of slow-motion by Penn and Peckinpah, then, we watch graceful women soar and spin in the air as they dispatch their adversaries (without the bloodshed of the earlier films) in lingering, drawn-out shots.

Structural

A second aesthetic use of violence occurs when it is used structurally, to shape the incidents of the movie story into an organic whole. Instead of a figurative rendering of a particular scene (as above), the violence contributes to the aesthetic unity of the entire cinematic experience. Marsha Kinder examines the way Sam Peckinpah, for instance, employs "violence to structure not merely individual sequences but the stylistic and narrative design of the entire film" (2001: 65). Peckinpah establishes the film's form in part by punctuating his traditional story-telling with bursts of violence, varying slow-motion and freeze-frame with real-time action. The violence becomes aesthetic by contributing to the rhythm and form of the film-story as a whole, as an organizing element in its larger aesthetic. As we shall see, such structuring is quite compatible with using the violence to also contribute to the meaning of the film-story.[1]

Narrative meaning

A third sense of aesthetic that contributes to the meaning of the film is found in the way it is essential to the import or sense of the film's narrative. In Stephen Teo's analysis of Hong Kong action films, both martial arts (*wuxia* – martial hero) and gangster (triad), the aesthetic aspect of film violence is found in its mythic significance for the narrative. Drawing on the work of Walter Benjamin, Teo argues that the concept of the mythic captures the most important sense of aesthetic cinematic violence. In mythical violence, humans come close to possessing divine power, but fall short due to human frailty (2011: 155). Teo understands mythic violence in action films as a critique of social institutions as forms of violence rather than as a challenge to violence *per se* (157). The aim of such mythically figured violence is inherently tied to law: whether reinforcing existing law or replacing it with improved versions. The mythologizing work of Hong Kong action movies is determined by the structure of their narratives in conjunction with scenes of divine-like destructive power. As with the organizational-structural sense of aesthetic violence, the narrative-meaning sense encompasses the film as a whole, but now in terms of thematic content rather than formal unity.

Peckinpah also uses his diverse shooting and editing techniques in this third aesthetic sense: to develop the meaning of the film-story. Among the techniques that Peckinpah employs to stylistically transform the violence is montage. Sometimes he will insert slow-motion shots into a traditional non-montage sequence; sometimes he will simply cut back and forth between different angles or perspectives during a violent incident. The resulting distortion of time can here suggest something about the meaning of the violence in the lives of the characters. Perhaps most relevant to augmenting the narrative meaning is Peckinpah's intercutting of flashbacks or parallel images to convey a character's thought or feeling. Such cutting follows what Stephen Prince calls a "psychologically poetic logic" (2003 : 87) By overlaying present action with earlier experiences of the character, the film rounds out the meaning of the violence for the character; the present can resonate with earlier friendship or failure, for instance, as it does in several of Peckinpah's Westerns. Although Peckinpah is certainly creating striking images and scenes that are detachable from the immediate narrative context, the aesthetic violence in many of these sequences also gives the narrative more depth (Prince 2003: 69–72) By cross-cutting scenes of the gang's history with occurring gunplay, for instance, Peckinpah elaborates on the sense in which its members subscribe to a code of honor in *The Wild Bunch.*

As indicated, these different senses of the aesthetic can be combined to powerful effect. An occurrence of violence that is symbolic can quite naturally be integral to the structure of the film-story. The twin ambushes in *Unforgiven* mentioned earlier work rhythmically with the scenes of violence that have preceded them (the slashing of the prostitute and thrashing of English Bob and Will Munny) as well as the climactic shoot-out that concludes the movie's action. For another example, the violence that exemplifies such figures as metalepsis or paradox, in our first sense of the aesthetic, can also contribute to the film-story's meaning. The stunning climax of *Bonnie and*

Clyde can be viewed as doing more than illustrating the contrast between the grace and the convulsions of the helpless body. As I suggested in the Introduction, the tableaux of the gangster couple battered by the overwhelming fusillade of bullets can also suggest their near-mythic, timeless notoriety. The cinematic immortalization captures the way in which Bonnie and Clyde fascinated the Depression-era country with their exploits. At the same time, their utter passivity during the ambush can allude to the fact that for all their derring-do, the pair was not truly in control of their destiny. Even as Arthur Penn shaped the scene and its shooting, so were the couple's actions and demise shaped by forces beyond their control or even understanding.

Aesthetic violence: formal-composition of scenes

As indicated, the aestheticization that characterizes the prior group of cinematic strategies can be understood as contributing to the conceptual or structural meaning of the film: it operates in the mode of making sense of the movie and its story. In contrast with these uses, the aestheticization that predominates the discussion of most of the book examines the composition of the violent movie action: the aesthetic here is understood in the mode of the formal-compositional. Aestheticized violence in this mode addresses the way the aesthetic qualities of images are accentuated, usually through technological sleight-of-hand. The aesthetic as formal-compositional zeroes in on hue and color saturation, modulation of line, form and style of movement: more traditional aesthetic qualities found, for example, in painting. Concern with realism is cast aside as the audience is brought under the spell of visually pleasing sequences created by cinemagraphic technologies such as slow-motion, reverse-motion, and digitization. The images considered here will be confined to the violence done directly by individuals to other people, not explosions, fireballs, earthquakes or the collapse of cities. Aestheticized personal violence in the movies features the sensuous qualities involved in direct physical conflict. In the following analysis of the ways in which film aestheticizes violence, a rough typology is proposed with an emphasis on what I construe as "surrealistic" violence.

Mega-violence

In characterizing three subgenres of cinematic violence I proceed from the least to the most aesthetically rich: extreme or mega-violence, hyper-violence, and surrealistic violence. The term "mega-violence" signifies great quantities or accumulations of violence. The prefix borrows from what have become standard uses: mega-ton bombs; mega-watt lights; huge consumer spaces that are mega-stores or mega-malls; and events that are so massive as to be "megaspectacles." Daniel Krier and William Swart characterize the bustling, carnivalesque productions of motorcycle rallies and stock-car races as megaspectacles and provide an illuminating socio-economic analysis of them (2017: 122–149). Although cinematic episodes of violence that are extreme may be offered and enjoyed for their own sake, the images themselves are not exceptional for their aesthetic features. For that reason mega-violence is minimally aesthetic. Extensive maiming or killing of people does not in itself involve fabricating images whose qualities aesthetically alluring. In mega-violence, such as found in many Schwarzenegger or John Woo films, the movie heaps great quantities of violence upon yet more violence. Increase in amount of blood-letting does not by itself produce transformation; quantitative expansion is not a qualitative reworking in the portrayal of violence.

Nevertheless, there can be an aesthetic aspect to sheer repetition, as in Andy Warhol's Campbell soup cans, a sea of cars on a dealership lot, or a herd of antelope. Voluminous violence can make an artful impact. Packing enormous carnage densely into a rapid sequence of shots or a short span of scenes can have an exhilarating effect. The cascade of wounding, blood-letting and killing can create the aesthetic forcefulness of the overwhelming, analogous to the way an avalanche of snow or recurring towers of tidal waves appear overpowering.[2]

Consider the landing on Omaha Beach on D-Day, early in *Saving Private Ryan* (Steven Spielberg, 1998). Hundreds of men are wounded or killed by gunfire and mortar. We see soldiers blown apart and into the air, limbs are shot off, entrails pour out. The air is thick with dirt, smoke, water spray and the sounds of bombardment and screaming men. Soldiers are set afire: first Americans during the amphibious landing, later Germans as the Americans advance. Another wartime sequence, also temporally extended, occurs in the climax of *Avatar* (James Cameron, 2009). Natives of the moon Pandora, the humanoid Na'vi, struggle to repel the invasive human army. In the ensuing battle, natives and earthlings kill one another in droves: in the air and on the land, with guns and arrows. The violence in these scenes is meant to be taken as realistic; what we see on the screen could conceivably look like this in the real world.

In both films, moreover, the extreme violence does not occur all at once, but accumulates, as if being tabulated on a mortality meter. By orchestrating the violence in waves, with periods of respite, films featuring mega-violence establish a percussive rhythm. So, too, can films increase the mega-violence in a given sequence, or over the course of the entire story, to a crescendo. Escalating violence clearly is more stirring than violence that diminishes or plateaus. Both the rhythmic and crescendoing arrangements can add an aesthetic layer to the mere accumulation of the piled on violence. Consequently, extreme violence in film can occupy a place bordering on more artfully aestheticized violence.

Hyper-violence

In contrast with mega-violence are two modes of movie destruction that do reconfigure physical conflict through cinematic manipulation to artistic effect. In hyper- and surrealistic violence, the visual displays can be appreciated independent of the trajectory of the story-line, as if viewed in an art gallery or museum. Hyper-violence plays with the sensuous surface of human destruction in visually compelling ways. It may include great magnitude, but it is not simply more of the same. As with mega-violence, the characters behave in relatively realistic fashion. The actions of the characters are not beyond the reach of ordinary (albeit athletic) individuals; swinging a sword or throwing a knife the way the characters do could be accomplished in the real world. However, the consequences of these actions, their drawn-out visual effects, could not be perceived in everyday life, as they require the artifice of the movie-maker. The slow-motion severing of an arm or the spreading of pulsing blood can only be produced by means of camera-work or film-editing. The violence can be considered "hyper" because it is above and beyond the simple excesses of realistic representations (including those found in mega-violence); it is hyperbolic in exaggerating images of the physical destruction. Hyper-violence intensifies the effects of bodily onslaught, for example, by enlarging the spatter of blood or dwelling on its pattern.

The film *Django Unchained* (Quentin Tarantino, 2012) offers two scenes of hyper-violence, the first of which is a short, understated prelude to the more kinetic, second episode. In it, a man riding on horseback in a sunny countryside is shot with a rifle. We see the blood that spurts out his back immediately stipple white cotton balls. The crimson flecks are beautiful against their puffy, miniature clouds of cotton. Later, the hyper-violence shifts indoors, to the darkened interior of the plantation's mansion. A man is shot and as he goes flying through a doorway into the air, blood is sprayed from his body. The title character leaps backward from the same doorway, lands on the slain man's back, and shoots another antagonist with his handgun, releasing a second red mist. The first victim, lying on the ground, is accidentally shot by one of his confederates, and emits more blood splatter. Amidst a barrage of rifle and handgun fire, Django's bullets propel thick plumes of blood from of a series of his attackers. In this extended scene of hyper-violent havoc, the opening sprays of blood serve as the first stage leading up to the more saturated, dense globs and fans of red bodily fluid – much as the earlier scene of blood-flecked cotton balls anticipates this broader and more intense array of killing. The almost tranquil, airy outdoor shooting of one rider and its prettified aftermath contrast dramatically with the shadowy, interior rapid-fire destruction of more than a dozen gunmen.

Surrealistic violence

In surrealistically crafted violence, the actions themselves are not possible in real life; they defy the laws of gravity as well as the limits of the human body. Moreover, bloodshed and bodily trauma are elided in favor of graceful movement and creative playfulness. Surrealistic violence involves a greater break with realism (with a correlative elevating of the aesthetic) through its more elaborate transformation of violence. The violent action is transfigured into aerial dance. As a result, the ugliness of fighting is transcended rather than sublimated (as in the metonymy described by Stephen Prince), over-come rather than folded under. The contrast that Lisa Stokes and Michael Hoover draw between typical Jackie Chan (non-surrealistic) films and standard action movies captures this important characteristic of surrealistic violence. They note that "while the characters in a [Jackie] Chan fight rarely suffer serious injuries (in fact, there is often an absence of blood), the physical punishment in a [Stephen] Seagal picture is graphically depicted" (1999: 243).

Emphasizing the subtlety, precision and elegance of the best martial arts movies, David Bordwell contrasts them with the more crude presentations of films that depict mega-violence: a particular sequence in *Righting Wrongs* (Yuen Kuei, 1986) "puts to shame the storyboard fights in big-budget Schwarzenegger films, where firepower substitutes for briskness and finesse" (2000a: 243). Although not focused on surrealistically portrayed violence, Bordwell's observations seem to apply most fittingly to them. Seeking to explain why *wuxia pian* films are especially exhilarating, he notes that the films pull us in by offering "us the illusion of mastering the action . . . the very cogency of the presentation has invited us to feel something of what supreme physical control might be like" (244). Similarly impressed by the infectious force of aesthetically rendered martial arts sequences, L. S. Kim remarks that "the viewer feels empowered, enabled, and elated" (2006). Surely of all martial arts films, those which depict violence surrealistically in defiance of everyday bodily limitations most fully realize Bordwell's exaltation, that "in the best Hong Kong sequences, we rejoice in cinema's power over the physical world" (245).

Elements of surrealistic violence are found in a film that can plausibly be seen as a precursor to the martial arts films that are here taken to be paradigms of the surrealistic subgenre. In addition, *A Touch of Zen* (King Hu, 1971) also anticipates the elevation of women in such cinema – both off the ground and into starring roles. Tellingly, the title in Mandarin is literally translated as "hero woman." As Stephen Teo is quick to point out, Hu is a pioneer of the lady knight-errant (*xia nu*) as the equal of or superior to her male counterparts in fighting prowess (2000). Although the film-story tends to drag, meander and move fitfully, its plot and thematic core anticipate more recent films. The central martial arts practitioner (Yang) is female; she is an insurgent against the established male forces of oppression; and both she and her male confederate (General Shi) start out in disguise.

The film also presents action that (in retrospect) seems to be an incipient version of surrealistic battle. We watch as Yang and Shi make impossible bounce-leaps and somersaults, vaulting effortlessly over walls and fallen enemies. Presaging by some thirty years the bamboo forest conflict in *House of Flying Daggers* (Zhang Yimou, 2004), combat occurs aloft in the trees and Yang descends, flying from atop a stand of trees. During one skirmish, the Chief Commander of the enemy forces leaps from the trees, and caroms off trunks – spinning and wheeling. As if to underscore the liberation of the heroine from traditional roles, the baby Yang produces is given over to the care of its father, the painter Gu. The role reversal frees Yang to live on her own or with the Buddhist monks who have protected her and taught her martial arts. As we will see, the heroines in the more recent films of surrealistic violence similarly eschew traditional family roles in an attempt to define themselves anew.

A major difference between *A Touch of Zen* and the films celebrating surrealistic violence that I investigate is the way in which the latter portray gravity-defying action. In the more recent films, the directors can avail themselves of technological advances that allow a full-frame or long-shot representation of the bounding, soaring, gyrating or somersaulting prowess. Relying on his wiles of camera-work and editing, King Hu had to imply more than depict the fantastic movement. Perfecting what David Bordwell calls "elliptical editing," Hu permits the audience "only a trace of the warriors' amazing feats. We do not see the action so much as glimpse it" (Bordwell 2000b: 119).

During the long, final battle in the glade, in *A Touch of Zen*, Hu suggests spectacular movement through an exit/entry pattern of cutting.

> Shi falls back and starts to struggle up to the left. An enemy swordsman descends upon him. In the next shot, the swordsman is leaping rightward out of the frame. Into the blank frame Shi rises and slashes right. In an instant the fighters have traded places, while the cuts reveal images that cannot hold them for very long.

(123)

The result of making the battle exploits so captivating in their fabulous execution is that the scenes themselves take on an intrinsic value. A tendency that Bordwell attributes to Hu finds full-flowering in the surrealistic subgenre: "Hu moves toward a kind of pure cinema, in which the pattern and pacing of the images command attention as much as the story action" (Bordwell 2000b: 132). It is like reveling in the poetic speech of a character in a Shakespearean drama at the same time that we grasp its import for and in the overall drama.

There are several other narrative aspects of the surrealistic action film beside lack of injury and bloodshed that buttress its aesthetic elegance. As a concomitant of the absence of injury and gore, the combatants naturally show little pain while giving and taking an enormous number and variety of blows. In addition, the combatants are usually relatively evenly matched: either two comparable fighters or one superior fighter taking on a throng of enemies. Moreover, the protagonist almost always does her violence in self-defense rather than as an aggressor. These last two aspects of the surrealistically violent hero(ine) support the rightness of her violence; it is more justified than that of her antagonists (Arons 2001: 31).

There is always the danger of misunderstanding when a term with a notable history of meaning is modified for a new purpose. Beginning as an innovation in painting during the 1920s, Surrealism had the proclaimed goal of transposing dreams "directly from unconscious mind to the canvas" (Janson 1962: 530). Surrealists broke with conventionally realistic modes of representation in an attempt to tap into the deeper layers of primitive and symbolic meaning purportedly pursued by psychoanalysis. Artists such as Max Ernst experimented with techniques to maximize the results of chance and Salvador Dali sought dream-like effects with such images as apparently melting watches in his now classical "The Persistence of Memory" (1931). With *The Andalusian Dog* (1929) and *The Age of Gold* (1930), Dali continued his surrealistic venture by collaborating in movie-making with director Luis Bunuel. Among more celebrated recent film directors considered surrealistic is David Lynch. Besides creating psychologically disturbing stories, Lynch fractures or otherwise disrupts narrative continuity in such works as the television series *Twin Peaks* (1990–91) and film *Mulholland Drive* (2001). These comments do little more than indicate the contours and texture of surrealism in the arts, but they should provide a workable context for the use of the term here.

As used in my analysis of cinematic violence, the term shares with Surrealism reference to exotic imagery, currents of enchantment, and the haunting portrayal of otherwise commonplace things. The dream-like quality of some of the film scenes examined also intimate regions of symbolic meaning, including symbols that penetrate the very experience of filmed violence with which audiences have grown familiar. But surrealistic movie violence favors the fantastic and lyrical instead of the macabre or chilling as found in Dali and Bunuel or Lynch. The poetic movement of the female protagonists, however, can muffle their archetypal yearnings as well as the social bondage which can be as symbolically disfiguring as the more overt, literal disfigurement of the sliced eyeball with which Dali and Bunuel introduce *The Andalusian Dog.* The needs of women and their social constraints are also more pivotal than found in more standard action films. These major themes will be developed in the analysis of the pair of films that epitomize surrealistic violence: *Crouching Tiger, Hidden Dragon* (Ang Lee, 2000) and *House of Flying Daggers* (Zhang Yimou, 2004).

The term that Wendy Arons uses to capture the features I construe as surrealistic is helpful. She distinguishes these films from other martial arts fare as "fantasy-action." The fantasy-action film is characterized "By its extreme stylization and its use of special effects to evoke a world of supernatural powers, magical weapons, and mysterious, mystical forces and energies" (2001: 27–51). A world of stylized violence and supernatural powers will quite naturally push narrative interpretation in one direction rather than another, suggesting various themes and meanings that would be less salient in more conventionally wrought martial arts movies.

Formal-composition and meaning combined

These three species of compositional-aesthetic violence are usually informed by the first types of aestheticization, those that operate in the mode of meaning or overall structure. In other words, the two modes (or axes) of aesthetic violence can and do dialectically modify one another. For example, shots of hyper-violence can also function symbolically. The blood-spotted balls of cotton in *Django Unchained* can plausibly be interpreted as symbolizing the fact that the boon of cotton as a cash crop is made possible by the blood of black slaves. Similarly, extreme or mega-violence often helps structure the film-story or is essential to its narrative meaning. The mega-violence that saturates the finale of the film *Avatar*, for instance, completes the plot by enabling the human hero to become transformed into a native Na'vi; moreover, the violence and its aftermath fulfill the narrative meaning of the story by supplanting the imperialistic ambitions of earth with the peaceful ethos of Pandora.

Surrealistic violence can also function metaphorically. In *Crouching Tiger, Hidden Dragon,* for another example, women are denied the independence needed to choose the life they wish, including the life of a martial arts warrior. Family customs, law, social norms and especially the engrained expectations of men stifle the aspirations of the protagonist and her would-be mentor. The surrealism of the film's violence involves leaping, tumbling, spinning and flying through air. It is most conspicuously and artfully performed by women. Through the magic of cinematography and editing, women disarm and dispose of dozens of male antagonists in gravity-defying elegance, but with neither the muscular nor bloody display of traditional male-centered combat. The intermittent freedom of women from the force the earth exerts on their bodies during their flights of surrealistic violence can be interpreted as a metaphor for their temporary freedom from the social forces that weigh them down psychologically and socially.

The surrealistic violence can also contribute to the meaning of the film-story in a more pervasive manner. To the soaring and leaping of *Crouching Tiger, Hidden Dragon* is added surrealistic treatment of weaponry in *House of Flying Daggers*. Slow-motion shots of the famous daggers performing impossible feats add to the otherworldly quality of the martial arts sequences. The plot of the film-story revolves around a secret band of warrior women in rebellion against male military and political rule. That they defeat the male soldiers without blood or gore, moreover, suggests that their opposition to male dominance includes a subversive, oppositional violence that is non-destructive. The surrealistic violence of the women can be understood as representing the assertion of women over their oppressors in a transformed and transformative way: without recourse to the brutality that has been visited on them. Combat and, by implication, rule by women is to be characterized by a form of force that does not dehumanize when it subdues.

Of course, films that showcase surrealistic violence need not, and have not, always featured warrior women as the central characters. Conversely, women can be and are the action heroes in films (such as *Salt* and *Kill Bill*) in which the violence is not rendered in a surrealistic way. Nevertheless, in Chapters 4 and 5 I shall argue that there is an affinity between women and surrealistic violence that is like the affinity, say, between dance and music or mathematics and chess. Explaining how women have arrived as the driving force of so many recent action movies is the task of the next chapter.

Notes

1 Some years ago, I wrote about the aesthetic nature of the "ultra-violence" of Stanley Kubrick's *A Clockwork Orange* (1971). Although used to structure the film-story and give meaning to it, ultra-violence as I conceived it was violence that was enjoyed for its aesthetic qualities by the characters (or one character, Alex) *within* the film. Alex is depicted as appreciating ultra-violence for its bloody hue and kinetics. However, the aesthetic enjoyment was not necessarily translated into an appreciation of the violence external to the story, for the audience, as it is with regard to the aesthetic violence discussed in this book.

2 In Immanuel Kant's classic discussion of the sublime, he divides the overwhelming experiences of nature into the mathematically sublime (great quantity) and the dynamically sublime (great force) (1987). My suggestion that great amounts of film violence can produce something like the overwhelming experience of natural sublimity can be viewed as combining the quantity of Kant's mathematical sublimity with the forcefulness of his dynamic sublimity.

Bibliography

Arons, Wendy (2001). "'If Her Stunning Beauty Doesn't Bring You to Your Knees, Her Deadly Drop Kick Will': Violent Women in the Hong Kong Kung Fu Film." *Reel Knockouts: Violent Women in the Movies*, Eds. M. McCaughey and N. King, pp. 27–51. Austin, TX: University of Texas Press.

Benjamin, Walter (1986). *Critique of Violence: Reflections: Essays, Aphorisms, Autobiographical Writings*, Ed. P. Demetz. New York: Schocken.

Bordwell, David (2000a). *Planet Hong Kong: Popular Cinema and the Art of Entertainment*. Cambridge, MA: Harvard University Press.

——— (2000b). "Richness through Imperfection: King Hu and the Glimpse." *The Cinema of Hong Kong: History, Arts, Identity*, Eds. P. Fu and D. Desser, pp. 113–37. Cambridge: Cambridge University Press.

Crowdus, Gary and Richard Porton (1993). "The Importance of a Singular guiding Vision: An Interview with Arthur Penn." *Cineaste*, 20, no.2, (spring), 12.

Janson, H.W. (1962). *History of Art*. Englewood Cliffs, NJ: Prentice-Hall.

Kant, Immanuel (1987). *Critique of Judgment*, Trans. Werner S. Pluhar. Indianapolis, IN: Hackett.

Kim, L.S. (2006). "*Crouching Tiger, Hidden Dragon*: Making Women Warriors: A Transnational Reading of Asian Female Action Heroes." *Jump Cut: A Review of Contemporary Media*, 48. www.ejumpcut.org/archive/Jc48.2006/WomenWarriors.

Kinder, Marsha (2001). "Violence American Style: The Narrative Orchestration of Violent Attractions." *Violence and American Cinema*, Ed. J. David Slocum, pp. 63–100. New York: Routledge.

Krier, Daniel, and William Swart (2017). *NASCAR, Sturgis, and the New Economy of Spectacle*. Austin: University of Texas.

Prince, Stephen (2003). *Classical Film Violence*. New Brunswick, NJ: Rutgers.

Stokes, Lisa, and Michael Hoover (1999). *City on Fire: Hong Kong Cinema*. London: Verso.

Teo, Stephen (2000). "Love and Swords: The Dialectics of Martial Arts Romance: A Review of *Crouching Tiger, Hidden Dragon*." *Sense of Cinema*. www.senseofcinema.com/2000/current-releases-11/crouching.

——— (2011). "The Aesthetics of Mythical Violence in Hong Kong Action Films." *New Cinema*, 8 (3), 155–67.

Filmography

Bunuel, Luis, and Salvador Dali (1929). *The Andalusian Dog*. Fr.

——— (1930). *The Age of Gold*. Fr.

Cameron, James (2009). *Avatar*. U.S.

Caton-Jones, Michael (1995). *Rob Roy*. U.S.
Eastwood, Clint (1992). *Unforgiven*. U.S.
Hawks, Howard (1932). *Scarface*. U.S.
Hu, King (1971). *Touch of Zen*. H.K.
Kloves, Steve (1989). *The Fabulous Baker Boys*. U.S.
Kubrick, Stanley (1971). *A Clockwork Orange*. U.S.
Kuei, Yuen (1986). *Righting Wrongs*. H.K.
Lee, Ang (2000). *Crouching Tiger, Hidden Dragon*. Taiwan, U.S., H.K., Ch.
Lynch, David (1990–91). *Twin Peaks*. U.S.
——— (2001). *Mulholland Drive*. U.S.
Morrison, Phil (2005). *Junebug*. U.S.
Noyce, Phillip (2010). *Salt*. U.S.
Peckinpah, Sam (1969). *The Wild Bunch*. U.S.
Penn, Arthur (1967). *Bonnie and Clyde*. U.S.
Spielberg, Stephen (1998). *Saving Private Ryan*. U.S.
Tarantino, Quentin (2003–04). *Kill Bill (Volumes I and II)*. U.S.
——— (2012). *Django Unchained*. U.S.
Yimou, Zhang (2004). *The House of Flying Daggers*. H.K. and China.

2 Women warriors

The rise of female control

The last several decades have moved women from peripheral roles in violent films to the center of the action and the story. As Marc O'Day graphically observes, "One of the most striking developments in recent popular cinema has been the wave of action-adventure films featuring attractive women stars as hugely capable heroines 'kicking ass' in a range of fantasy oriented screen worlds" (2004: 201). No longer an auxiliary to her more formidable male protagonist, the warrior woman enjoys "narrative 'prominence'" (Kim 2006). As suggested in the Introduction, *Bonnie and Clyde* (Arthur Penn, 1967) is a plausible place to see the shift begin. Not only is the violence more stylized and filled with greater anatomical detail than its predecessors, but a violent woman is pivotal to the action and plot (Kolker 1980: 52). It seems reasonable to think that without Bonnie the film would be simplified, flattened and much less interesting. One of the ways in which Bonnie's participation in the Barrow gang's escapades intensifies and enriches the film is by upending gender expectations. As Hilary Neroni contends, "Bonnie's violence represented an imbalance in the normal relationship between masculinity and femininity" (2005: 115). Coupled with Clyde's sexual shortcomings, Bonnie's aggressiveness bolsters her power and place in the film-story. Bonnie's enjoyment of the violence "undermines our traditional understanding of masculinity and femininity" (116). When women start taking charge in ways traditionally enjoyed by men, the meaning and norms associated with gender are bound to change.

Bonnie represents a sea change in the portrayal of women in film. A cold-blooded, female participant in outlaw violence who enjoys the chase, shoot-out and killing certainly cuts against the cinematic grain of portrayals of womanhood, even wicked or deadly ones. As groundbreaking as Arthur Penn's film was, it turned out to be but a nascent move in the direction of robust women warriors on screen. Bonnie remains an accomplice or sidekick to the male outlaw; she is romantically involved with him and is dependent on Clyde as both his girl and gunsel moll. As we will see, the female action hero evolves into a woman who breaks free of these character and plot constraints. Later women warriors will not be dependent on men and will not be their sidekicks or girlfriends. Romance will be as foreign to most of them as motherhood. They will further challenge standard male-female identity ascriptions in film by sporting muscles and displaying fighting prowess. They will vanquish men not just with guns, as Bonnie does, but by wielding swords and knives, and more intimately in hand-to-hand combat. What it is to be female will be challenged by these fighting women: first simply by their violence and their enjoyment of it, then by their brawn, and finally by their sexuality. These are the main themes to be explored in what follows.

Just as violence in the movies is a vast terrain, the rise of the woman warrior encompasses a panoply of topics and admits of a multiplicity of approaches. By necessity, many of these topics and approaches must be merely noted in passing or omitted altogether in the following overview. For example, because ethnicity and race are peripheral to my project, women in the Blaxploitation genre are not addressed as well they might be.[1] I also put to one side the important perspectives of politics, psychology and Asian identity as these are also tangential to the main interests of the book.[2] What I try to do is give the reader a sense of how the role of women in the presentation of cinematic violence has developed, giving special attention to various characters and actors that can serve as helpful points of popular reference.[3] The development of which I speak, however, refers to films that aim at a western or international audience. A majority of films in which violent women are the primary characters are either Hong Kong movies or are indebted to these movies, including the three films I treat as paradigms of aesthetic violence.

For the historical record, then, it is important to note that "Hong Kong action cinema has long created women warriors who fight men as equals" (Lo 2007: 126). Kwai-Cheung Lo proceeds to back up her claim by tracing female fighters much further back than the heralded heroines in the films of director King Hu, such as Cheng Pei-Pei (*Come Drink with Me*, 1966) and Hsu Feng (*A Touch of Zen*, 1971). Lo points out that Yu So-Chan "played various women warriors in low-budget Cantonese swordplay films since the late forties" (126). Earlier still was Xuan Jinglin in the silent film *The Nameless Hero* (Zhang Shichuan, 1926). Wendy Arons concurs with Lo, asserting that "The woman warrior in the kung fu film is thus by no means a new phenomenon, and from its very beginning the genre has featured women in heroic fighting roles" (2001: 31). Arons proceeds to cite the Peking Opera and the legend of the male martial arts expert Fong Sai Yuk who was trained by his mother in tracing the lineage of the woman warrior in Asian culture.[4] But what is nonetheless striking in cinema of recent vintage is the prominence of women as the leading characters in the film-stories, "as the central

visual and narrative driver within the overall audio-visual feast which contemporary action-adventure aims to offer its audience" (O'Day 2004: 207).
The discussion that follows concentrates on films made during the last several decades.

Defining features of action heroines

Linda Hamilton as Sarah Connor in *The Terminator* (James Cameron, 1984)
provides a fruitful example of a woman who is the focal point of a series of
violent films. First, it is important to note that as with several other violent
women, Connor is thrust into her role; it is forced upon her. This is a subtle
way in which the strong, independent fighting woman cinematically morphs
from more traditional, and safe, images of woman in the movies. Because
she is not in control of whether to assume the traditionally masculine role
of action hero, the woman warrior who is like Connor is initially a less for-
bidding figure than her male counterpart. On the other hand, because she is
able to transform herself and adapt – as Ripley also does in *Alien* (Ridley
Scott, 1979), for example – she displays an auxiliary strength usually absent
from male action heroes. Second, and consonant with the ability to reinvent
herself, is Connor's transition from someone (in *The Terminator*) who is
in need of male protection to a tough, confident combatant in *Terminator
2: Judgment Day* (James Cameron, 1991). Connor is athletic and ready for
battle, having "lost her maternal femininity," she "adapts a more masculine
persona (toting a gun with muscles bulging)" (Neroni 2005: 83–84). If her
strength and fortitude do not exactly replace her mothering side, they come
to the fore in its service and all but overshadow her nurturing nature.

Another notable departure for women in violent movies is their independence from men. They have little need for male help; whereas, male
violence has often been justified as necessary in order to protect women
(Neroni 2005: 92). Yvonne Tasker remarks that in their typical movie roles,
moreover, the vulnerability of women and their dependence on men functioned to emphasize the masculine identity of the male hero (1993: 28).
When women are no longer presented in this way, masculine identity and
its violence may be called into question. I will deal with this topic more
extensively in connection with the sexuality of the woman warrior. Indeed,
much of the violence of female action heroes is directed at men and can be
seen as the result of mistreatment at the hands of men. The female violence
that occurs in our *wuxia* films of surrealistic violence, for example, can be
understood as generated by the oppressive social conditions imposed by
the male hierarchy.

The independence of the woman warrior from men extends to the absence
of romantic involvement. The action heroine in *Rambo: First Blood Part II*

(George Cosmatos, 1985) does have a brief romantic moment with the title character; however Co Bao is quickly killed off. Yvonne Tasker thinks that romance for the action heroine "is a little too much for the film to deal with because the roles of fighting female and romantic girlfriend do not jibe . . . it is made clear that the two roles are incompatible, unable to exist simultaneously" (1993: 28). The absence of romantic union in films becomes the norm in film-stories in which violent women are predominant. Hilary Neroni finds the lack of romantic relationships "striking because a staple of Hollywood films, especially their conclusion" (2005: 85). It is as if the filmmakers feel the need to omit heterosexual involvement because it does not comport easily with a type of woman who deviates in such marked ways from the typical representation of women for whom romance was desirable. Once freed of her dependence on men, the fighting woman cannot be reconnected to them in a standard manner. Both of these aspects of women warriors characterize the protagonists in a landmark film featuring violent women: *Thelma and Louise* (Ridley Scott, 1991).

The violence of the title characters provides an impetus for them to break loose from the limitations imposed by their traditional roles as women. "After Thelma and Louise commit one violent act, they spend the rest of the film shedding their femininity" (Neroni 2005: 94). For instance, they replace emblems of their former gender-identification, remaking themselves with such trappings as cowboy hats, suitable for gun-toting gals on the lam. The suggestion is that violence precludes true or traditional femininity. They are also liberated from their domestic gender constraints such as the sexual submissiveness demanded by Thelma's husband. Shortly after *Thelma and Louise*, a female-centered martial arts film underscored the incompatibility between a woman's proficiency in battle and romantic involvement with a man. In *Naked Killer* ([Clarence] Fok Yiu-leung, 1992), Kitty is a desirable heterosexual woman who alone can restore the sexual potency of the policeman (Tinam). Yet her ally in combat, Cindy, tells her that she must give up being a professional assassin because a heterosexual love relationship would rob her of her female killer's power. Kitty does not, in fact, renounce her prowess in violence for a romantic attachment she desires; the film resolves the tension between these incompatible features of the violent woman by killing her off.

Another pivotal dimension of the violent woman as film protagonist is that she unleashes her destructive force in self-defense. Either she is attacked overtly by men who wish her harm or seek to violate her, or she is threatened more diffusely by the workings of a patriarchal social order. Addressing the violence of the female heroes of *Naked Killer*, Wendy Arons points out that they kill men only in self-defense: "we do not perceive Kitty and Cindy as malicious: their violence appears as a justifiable response to the pervasive threat of victimization" (2001: 36) But *Thelma and Louise* may seem to deviate from this sympathetic aspect of the warrior woman. The shooting and killing of the would-be rapist is somewhat gratuitous. Louise shoots him out of anger, when Thelma is no longer in danger. The shooting is symbolic and somewhat free. It makes Louise more dangerous and threatening, especially to men in the audience, because her violence seems unlimited and unpredictable since not tempered by the need to protect herself or Thelma.

Alternatively, the pair could also be viewed as provoked and killing in the face of the ubiquitous shadow of threat that men in general cast upon women. It is as if Thelma and Louise are symbolically sending a message to men who are not witnessing the scene, thereby bolstering their own courage and resolve. Understood in such a broader perspective, the apparently unnecessary killing of the assaulting man in the parking lot can also be cast as a form of revenge. Revenge is not simply for the attempted assault, which is past, but includes the systemic subjugation and humiliation of women, which is ongoing. The film vibrates with the excitement the friends feel at finally asserting themselves in response to the institutionalized oppression of women, embodied in Thelma's husband, the rapist, and later the sneering, supercilious truck driver.

Muscularity, masculinity and musculinity

In the evolution of the female action hero, she becomes more muscular, more like her masculine forerunners. Examining such action heroines as Sigourney Ripley in the *Alien* films and Linda Hamilton's portrayal of Sarah Connor in *The Terminator* franchise, Yvonne Tasker coins the term "musculinity" to capture the way cinematic emphasis on male musculature is now transferred to tough women. Moreover, these women deliver the same varieties of grisly destruction as the standard male heroes. Tasker thinks that masculinizing the female body is demanded by the narratives of these films as well as their male-centered tradition: "In order to function effectively within the threatening, macho world of the action picture, the action heroine must be masculinized" (1993: 149).

Nevertheless, the sexual aspect of these buff women is not always suppressed. Sometimes the films present tough women as also sexually appealing, and this can further upend gender norms and expectations. For example, Angelina Jolie as the title character in *Lara Croft: Tomb Raider* (Simon West, 2001) and in *Salt* (Phillip Noyce, 2010) not only kicks and punches with glistening muscles but is also sexual in her posture, movement and revealing costumes. Yet this too can be seen as reprising male-dominated violent movies, since the physiques and combative feats of men often positioned them as sexually attractive. However, the difference is that strength, power and fighting talent have not been typically associated with female sexuality. Although the *femme fatale* was exciting and somewhat exotic, because of the danger she posed, she was not physically the match of her male opponents or prey.[5] Until women were depicted as incarcerated for breaking the law or as law-enforcers, their skill lay more in manipulating men than in besting them in brawl: for example, Linda Fiorentino as Bridget Gregory in *The Last Seduction* (John Dahl, 1994) and Barbara Stanwyck as Phyllis Dietrichson in *Double Indemnity* (Billy Wilder, 1944). Indeed, the use of sexuality by these devious *femmes fatales* mirrored the brute strength of men in film as the alternative means for women getting what they wanted. When the action heroine has both muscles and sexual appeal (and sometimes the appeal is because of her muscularity), she occupies a novel place in film. I will return to the topic of sexuality in discussing the ways in which cinema contains or muffles the threat posed by women warriors.

Stephen Teo's mythic understanding of the aesthetic provides the framework for his interpretation of the action heroine. In Hong Kong films featuring women as "knights-errant," Teo writes, mythical violence becomes an expression of feminism, as gender stories of mythic violence "provide a critique of sexual norms in society" (2011: 161). Teo contends that the heroics of the female fighter challenge the social norms and roles assigned to women. Nevertheless, the female protagonists still perform in the mold of their male prototypes. Here Teo concurs with the position taken by Tasker, pointing out that the female knights carry guns and fight "with the same choreographic and stylish manner as their male counterparts do" (163). In struggling against the male version of symbolic violence, women wind up mirroring these traditional heroes of action cinema. When I examine the surrealistic action heroine in later chapters, I will show how she deviates from the muscularity of the Lara Crofts and Sarah Connors. The reconfiguration of the surrealistic female lead makes it all the more feasible to group realistic and hyper-violent action heroines with the brawny males whose appearance, attitude and action they emulate.

In the action film whose hero is male, the woman invariably plays a subordinate role, often being romantically (but not overtly sexually) involved with him. Drawing on quantitative, empirical research, Katy Gilpatric corroborates Tasker's claims to the effect that "female characters were masculinized when they engaged in violence" (2010: 736). Yet because the portrayal of these macho women is accompanied by "feminine stereotypes," according to Gilpatric, a tension results. The results of empirical research, notes Katy Gilpatric, indicate that female viewers are conflicted by erstwhile masculine violence performed by women who still conform to traditional understandings of womanhood. Gilpatric sees the findings as showing the "contradictory nature of female action characters in contemporary mainstream American cinema" (734).

Muscular women still possess female, sometimes feminine, attributes and this creates tension within the persona of these action heroines. Some theorists and empirical researchers construe the violent action woman in movies as "transgressive." The transgression results from the fact that the muscularity of action heroines is concomitant with their ascendance to film-story predominance. Conducting experiments with female viewers of *Thelma and Louise*, Tiina Vares found that the expectations and interpretations of the audience based on their experience with cinematic genres were frustrated. When women were the main protagonists, a "disruption of gendered conventions" occurred (2002: 216). Vares argues that important cinematic boundaries are crossed once killer women are "positioned at the center of both narrative knowledge and action and, as such, indicate various transgressions against the conventions of a number of action-based genres" (213).

Tasker agrees that because the action heroine "commands the narrative," various cinematic norms and expectations are upended. No longer highly sexualized (in the old-fashioned, feminine ways) as such action heroines as Charlie's Angels, the new violent women have usurped the place formerly enjoyed by the male hero. "At the most fundamental level, images of the active heroine disrupt the conventional notion . . . [to represent women] exclusively through the codes of femininity" (1993: 132). Theorists can also speculate about the effects of such transgressive or disruptive representations of women on movie-goers as well as on various art forms. For example, are violent female protagonists perceived as empowering to women and do they in fact empower women in their ordinary lives? Do women warriors simply reproduce the violence that has traditionally been the province of men and thereby work against genuinely liberating portrayals of women? I leave to one side the implications of various depictions of the action heroine for women and men once the movie-going is over. However, I will address such issues within the meaning of the films when discussing the depictions of women fighters performing feats of surrealistic violence.

Gender and power: tensions and resolutions

Muting the threat

What is important for my purposes is to investigate the tensions, if not conflict, between women as combatants and traditional norms of gender within the film-story. This includes how the relationship between the sexuality of the woman warrior and her fighting prowess might bear on her identity as a woman. Here different answers or interpretations may depend on how the violent woman is portrayed on screen and who the actress is. When the woman's violence is packaged with the brawn or sinew typically sported by male protagonists, of course, interpretations must take this added dimension into account.

By exaggerating their attractiveness and desirability as women, female action heroes simultaneously fit familiar images of women but also grate against them. As indicated above, one response is simply to be unsettled by the combination of femininity, including sexual attributes, and physical prowess. It does not compute. We can think of this as the "incongruity" view: the disruption of norms that define gender created by female violence makes it unacceptable. Because violence does not dovetail with what is understood to be a woman, it is dismissed as cinematic contrivance. The fighting, buff woman who does not need a man and is not romantically attached to one is an anomaly – like a vicious 2-year-old or a talking fish. As Kwai-Cheung Lo observes, "When the female protagonist gains extraordinary power or strength she can no longer be her original self as a daddy's girl, submissive wife or desirable girlfriend for men" (2007: 130). The discord or tension in ascertaining just who or what the female action hero is results from the way she upsets conventional gender roles.

An offbeat and complex example of disrupted gender identity is found in Stephen Chow's *Kung Fu Hustle* (2005). The film centers around "an unattractive, middle-aged, dumpy and bullying landlady (played by Yuen Qin)" (Lo 2007: 130). As the antithesis of the sexy tough combatant, the landlady hides her kung fu expertise and fights with her husband, who is also a martial arts adept. Although the female, aging warrior sides with the good characters against the villain, "she also upsets the conventional gender role: she is neither a virtuous motherly protector or a vicious femme fatale. This construction exposes contradictions within the gender dichotomy" (2007: 130–131). Lo finds that the fighting female cannot be construed as whole. Not only does Chow's character escalate the antagonisms between men and women created and perpetuated by the attractive fighting woman, but she seems to complicate the "antagonistic split within" the fighting woman's identity (131).

Despite the appeal of simply ending reflection by accepting the incongruity view of the competing factions of female identity, various attempts can be made to reconcile them within traditional frameworks of gender and sexuality. One such approach involves defining the female fighter as a masculine or masculinized woman. On this view, her apparent womanhood is subordinated to her masculine-looking physique and expertise at combat. Such a character is no longer disturbing or beyond the pale because she is slotted into the familiar category of butch. A paradigm of such a character is the soldier Private Vasquez (Jenette Goldstein) in *Aliens* (James Cameron,

1986) who has short hair, repeatedly flexes her muscles, indulges in male-shaped derogatory humor, and fancies herself "one of the boys." Audiences are liable to be relatively comfortable with this identity precisely because it resolves the apparent conflict between gender and violence, or gender and muscular violence.

However, the redefinition of the woman due to her violence may be so extreme as to be alarming. Where Vasquez's self-understanding and subsequent behavior align her with tough men, a pair of violent lesbians in *Naked Killer* kill men for the fun of it. Princess and Baby are man-hating, masculine women who not only castrate and kill men, but imitate the worst of men by raping women. The contrast between the masculinity represented by Vasquez and that found in Princess and Baby suggests that even when the violence of the action female remakes her into a pseudo-man, the result requires further differentiation: between the more socially acceptable (because protective) butch and the deviant, dangerous attack-bitch.

The most reactionary or conventional cinematic approach to strong women is to mute or modulate the threat they pose by offsetting their strength and fighting skill with attributes that are familiarly feminine. One way of softening the physical prowess of the female protagonist is through "narrative containment." Lisa Purse notes that the physically powerful woman can be reined in by the story-line in much the same way as socially dominant women were in such screwball comedies as *Bringing Up Baby* (Howard Hawks, 1938) and *The Awful Truth* (Leo McCarey, 1937): "The narrative containment of women often takes the form of a movement into, or a return to, the heterosexual couple, to marriage, or to the family unit (or all three), a strategy that gives the lie to the independence these powerful women appear to embody" (2011: 85). Domesticating the action heroine's potentially alarming violent talents normalizes her by inscribing the woman in a familiar gendered role, one that is endorsed and enforced by men.

A second way of balancing or offsetting the toughness of the action heroine with a familiar and desirable feminine attribute is, as we have seen, to accentuate her sexuality. As Stephanie Mencimer perceives her, "The new action babes have to celebrate women's power without being so threatening that men would be afraid to sleep with the leading lady" (2001: 18). On this interpretation, the sexuality of the woman warrior mitigates her violence so that she is still acceptable as a genuine woman. Once their sexuality is exaggerated (often through provocative costuming), female action heroes are normalized by conforming to the expectations derived from the "fetishistic figure of fantasy derived from comic books and soft pornography" (Tasker 1998: 69). Citing such characters as Angelina Jolie as Salt and Jennifer Garner as the title character in *Elektra* (Rob Bowman, 2005), Lisa Purse argues that "all these action heroines are displayed in ways that eroticise their gendered form – often precisely at the same moments they are demonstrating their active, capable physicality" (2011: 79). Marc O'Day notes how Jolie's blatant sexuality cues the audience for further titillation in *Lara Croft: Tomb Raider* with "an early teaser shower scene in which the heroine is unrobed, Lara turning coquettishly to one side to reveal the outline of her left breast" (2004: 214).[6]

The Hong Kong film *The Heroic Trio* (Johnnie To, 1992) provides an example of a whole team of action heroines whose supernatural fighting powers are offset by gendered attributes. Wendy Arons observes that the film goes to great lengths "to mitigate and neutralize the threat of female power by framing the women as sex objects" (2001: 40). The women are provocatively costumed so as to provide an "ostentatious display of breasts, legs, and buttocks," thereby muting the "impact of their display of violence" (41). Yet to further contain the threatening prowess of the trio the film supplements their blatant sexuality with carefully placed vulnerability. Their vulnerability is specifically tied to their gender, for example, by playing on their maternal instincts or concern with facial beauty. As Craig Reed points out, the fearless, skilled, aggressive women are depicted "with just enough vulnerability so that they don't threaten the very fabric of their chauvinistic Chinese society" (1997).

This manner of coming to terms with the apparent tension posed by the strong, violent woman reverses the "butch" interpretation; the desirable sexuality on the part of the woman dampens her violence instead of the violence redefining the woman's sexuality. But despite their apparent opposition, both the sexuality-as-compensation view and the woman-as-masculine understanding are fundamentally alike: both reconcile or dissolve the tension between womanhood and violence. By doing so, these perspectives are reassuring and avoid a deeper reconceptualization of the relationship between the woman's sexuality and her toughness. The next two interpretations, on the other hand, respond to the challenge of grappling with this tension in a new way, going beyond formulations that allow comfortable categorization.

Redefining gender

Hilary Neroni's approach to the apparent incompatibility between womanhood and violence is to suggest that it promotes gender fluidity; it opens up conceptual space for redefining what it is to be both a woman and a man. Neroni argues that the traditional complementarity between the sexes is undermined when women are violent. By subverting this complementarity, violent women in film open up possibilities for new gender definitions (2005: 93). But the traditional gender identity of women and men are mutually supportive: woman's dependence and weakness (including meekness) reinforces male dominance (including violence). Consequently, the fluidity of female gender definition implies a corresponding porousness in male identity: "Violence and femininity so contrast with each other that together they highlight the contingency of feminine identity, and therefore the contingency of the masculine identity as well" (95).[7]

Neroni's position means that norms governing female gender can be revised, enlarged or reshaped so as to find toughness, even muscularity, consonant with being female. Whether this includes her traditional sexuality is another question. One relatively early example of this is the female action protagonist, the muscular Mace (Angela Bassett), who repeatedly saves her friend Lenny (Ralph Fiennes) from physical harm in *Strange Days* (Katherine Bigelow, 1995). Such reversal of traditional gender roles, of course, includes the man being dependent on the woman's physical prowess for safety and even survival. Mace deals with danger calmly and wittily, but the fact that she is black and Lenny is white may make the relationship so anomalous as to erode the gender redefinition. In support of Neroni's contention, however, I think the racial mix can be seen as buttressing the gender fluidity. Not only can women be strong, stronger than men, but they can cross color lines in protecting them. After all, we rarely see inter-racial couples in which the female is both black and powerful. When we do, therefore, the upending of gender norms is reinforced by scrambling race norms.[8]

An alternative to the fluidity interpretation of female violence that also pursues the reconceptualization of gender is one that finds women warriors breaking new ground by incorporating or "straddling" both genders. Where the butch interpretation dissolved the traditional female attributes in a muscularized version of women and the compensatory interpretation muted the toughness with female sexuality, the combinational view keeps both in play. Jeffrey Brown argues that Pamela Anderson as the title character of *Barb Wire* (David Hogan, 1996) may be an extreme as a fetishistic fantasy figure but is no different in kind from all action heroines who reveal or excite "the adolescent fear and desire of female sexuality" (2004: 50). Brown thinks that virtually all violent film stars are not so much masculinized women as representatives of the iconic dominatrix. The exaggerated sexuality of women such as Pamela Anderson works with, not against, their toughness. The "Bad Girl" is complicated and complicates our response to her violence because she embodies both genders. If her female attractiveness were swallowed up in or by her masculinity, she would be easier to categorize as a masculine woman. Traditional gender definitions and constraints would hold. Instead, "Bad girl bodies are presented as dangerous not just because they can fight or shoot but because they are alluring" (65).

Brown's interpretation of the action heroine emphasizes that she embodies something new, a person who goes beyond typical gender norms, but does not thereby fall outside them – the easier or less complex way of going outside such norms. Brown offers the notion of "straddling" gender roles and norms rather than obliterating or discarding them: "the tough action heroine is a transgressive character not because she operates outside of gender restrictions, but because she straddles both sides of the . . . gender divide. She is both subject and object . . . ass kicker and sex object" (52). Protagonists who are merely masculinized (or muscularized) women are surely transgressive by defying the received understanding of what it is to be a woman or a successful woman. However, when they also possess erotic attributes (such as long legs, large breasts or sexy hair), the transgression is extended: the traditional understanding of gender is further undermined.

In providing an extension or revision of gender through the action heroine, another early (Hong Kong) film offers a still more radical alternative to Brown's straddling. In *Swordsman II* (Ching Siu-Tung and Stanley Tong 1992), Asia (Brigitte Lin Ching Hsia) is castrated in order to be transformed into a woman with supernatural powers. "The film thereby . . . represents the violent woman as a transformed man" (Arons 2001: 39). So far, this would be but an extreme version of the "butch" solution to the tension between violence and womanhood, as embodied by Private Vasquez in *Aliens*. However, once castrated Asia is not able to function sexually as a woman either. Instead of the heroine straddling two genders, as Brown interprets such woman warriors as Barb (Wire), Asia obliterates gendered identity and becomes something else altogether. Wendy Arons expresses Asia's status this way: "The violent woman is, in the end, a noncreature who is both man and woman – and neither" (39). Stephen Teo also views Asia as

> a new type of hero/heroine, a gender-bending character so malleable that he or she bends not only gender, but all character types: Asia is a villainess, a romantic protagonist, and ultimately a character who wins the sympathy of the hero – and the audience.
>
> (1997: 201)

More recently, violent film subverts the norms of femininity in yet another way. In the film *Hanna* (Joe Wright, 2011), for example, the title character is youthful as well as female. A sylph-like, young teen, Hanna (Saoirse Ronan) has been genetically engineered and then instructed (in the wilds of Finland) to be an ideal assassin; smart, strong, coordinated, quick, and fast, Hanna is not heavily muscled yet defeats her larger antagonists at every turn. As with the new adult warrior woman, Hanna does not have romantic interests, but she defies norms of childhood as well as those of femininity.

The film thereby provides a double reversal by making its female action star a waif-like girl. *Hanna* also resembles one of our paradigms of surrealistically violent films by pitting the girl against a dominant woman. Although Hanna spends most of her time running from, fighting off and defeating male adversaries, her nemesis is Marissa (Cate Blanchett), and we know from early in the film that the final showdown will require Hanna to vanquish her sole, female foe.

Positioning women as the main protagonists in violent film-stories subordinates men, but in a different way than women had been formerly subordinated – as sidekicks or love interests. Now, the men are prelude or ancillary to all-woman combat because these women are more formidable than their male counterparts: tougher, smarter, more determined and resourceful. True enough, Hanna had been trained by a man, Eric (her surrogate father); however, in *Crouching Tiger, Hidden Dragon*, one of our surrealistic mainstays, even this role has been taken over by a woman.

Playing the Bride in the pair of *Kill Bill* movies, Uma Thurman embodies many of the features that characterize warrior women. Most blatantly, she shows off muscular arms and legs, often glistening with perspiration, as she does battle with men and women alike. The Bride is nevertheless sexually appealing, and viewers can decide for themselves whether her impressive deltoids and swordplay contribute to it. To what extent do the Bride's masculine contours and conflicts compromise her femininity? Well, we are shown that all her personal relationships are problematic. So far from having a satisfying relationship with the man who has fathered her child, the Bride kills him, but only after he has barely failed to end her own life. Then, too, there is the question of the action hero's relationships with other women warriors. The story of *Kill Bill* consists largely in a skein of episodes aimed at avenging the treachery the Bride's former female comrades visited upon her. The ending of the Bride's tale leaves us wondering whether a woman whose adult life has been dedicated to killing is capable of transforming herself into a nurturing mother. The question is vivified by virtue of the large-scale, hyper-violent battle the Bride has had to win in order to arrive at her challenging moment of parenthood.

Notes

1 See Yvonne Tasker (1993), for a thumbnail sketch of strong women in Blaxploitation films, 21–23; and Hilary Neroni (2005), 27–33.
2 For instance, L.S. Kim suggests that "the Asian female action hero has functioned as an allegory asserting Hong Kong identity" (2006). She also asks whether U.S. viewers "are able to read women warriors through a Chinese cultural context. . . . Does pleasure come *in* the female action hero (identifying with or affirming their subjectivity), or *of* the 'battling babes' (ultimately objectifying them)?" Instead

of addressing these sorts of intriguing questions, I follow the lead of Martha McCaughey and Neal King, when they write, "It's not the business of analysts to decide which images will suit sexist reaction and which feminist revolution, which express dominance and which resistance" (2001: 2).

3 I should also note that I will not be exploring the action heroine in such media as comic books, video games or television, despite many connections between these vehicles and cinema.

4 In the legend of Wing Chun, for another example, a heroic woman is taught martial arts by another woman – a Buddhist nun: L.S. Kim (2006).

5 Hilary Neroni locates the classic femme fatale within film noir. Although defying a rigid definition, the femme fatale possesses: "a self-centered nature, an overt sexuality, and an ability to seduce and control almost any man who crosses her path" (2005: 22). For a helpful extended discussion of this type of dangerous woman and her connection with the violent females that are the subject of this book, see 19–33.

6 O'Day (2004: 215) goes on to explain the complexity of the allure of Jolie/Croft:

> Lara Croft as cinematic action babe heroine echoes many iconic figures from the action-adventure tradition: she is a bit James Bond (neo-imperialist agent), Indiana Jones (archaeologist adventurer), Batman (has an estate and an eccentric butler), and Tarzan (swings from ropes and dives off waterfalls), and a bit of Modesty Blaise, Barbarella and Tank Girl.

7 Neroni maintains that beneath the surface of the old-fashioned, complementary understanding of the sexes there often simmered conflict between screen men and women. Among the possibilities opened up by violent women, Neroni sees the opportunity for exposing "latent antagonism between men and women" (93).

8 It should be added that the film ends with Mace and Lenny in a romantic clinch. The repositioning of the strong woman within the familiar confines of a heterosexual relationship may in fact soften her otherwise exceptional role as champion and protector.

Bibliography

Arons, Wendy (2001). "'If Her Stunning Beauty Doesn't Bring You to Your Knees, Her Deadly Drop Kick Will': Violent Women in the Hong Kong Kung Fu Film." *Reel Knockouts: Violent Women in the Movies*, Eds. M. McCaughey and N. King, pp. 27–51. Austin, TX: University of Texas Press.

Brown, Jeffrey (2004). "Gender, Sexuality, and Toughness: The Bad Girls of Action Film and Comic Books." *Action Chicks: New Images of Tough Women in Popular Culture*, Ed. S. Inness, pp. 47–74. New York: Palgrave Macmillan.

Gilpatric, Katy (2010). "Violent Female Action Characters in Contemporary American Cinema." *Sex Roles*, 62, 734–46.

Kim, L.S. (2006). "*Crouching Tiger, Hidden Dragon*: Making Women Warriors: A Transnational Reading of Asian Female Action Heroes." *Jump Cut: A Review of Contemporary Media*, 48. www.ejumpcut.org/archive/Jc48.2006/WomenWarriors.

Kolker, Robert (1980). *A Cinema of Loneliness: Penn, Kubrick, Coppola, Scorsese, Altman*. New York: Oxford.

Lo, Kwai-Cheung (2007). "Copies of Copies." *Hong Kong Film, Hollywood and the New Global Cinema*, Eds. G. Marchetti and T. See Kam, pp. 126–36. London: Routledge.

McCaughey, Martha and Neal King (2001). *Reel Knockouts: Violent Women in the Movies*, Austin, TX: University of Texas Press.

Mencimer, Stephanie (2001). "Violent Femmes." *Washington Monthly*, Sept., 2001, 15–18.

Neroni, Hilary (2005). *The Violent Woman: Femininity, Narrative, and Violence in Contemporary Action Cinema*. Albany, NY: SUNY Press.

O'Day, Marc (2004). "Beauty in Motion: Gender, Spectacle and Action Babe Cinema." *Action and Adventure Cinema*, Ed. Yvonne Tasker, pp. 201–18. London: Routledge.

Purse, Lisa (2011). *Contemporary Action Cinema*. Edinburgh: Edinburgh University Press.

Reed, Craig (1997). "Those Wild Women of Fant-Asia." *Boxoffice Magazine* (Special Report, Mar. 25, 1997). www.boxoff.com/sneak2bfeb.html.

Tasker, Yvonne (1993). *Spectacular Bodies: Gender, Genre and the Action Cinema*. New York and London: Routledge.

Teo, Stephen (1997). *Hong Kong Cinema: The Extra Dimensions*. London: British Film Institute.

——— (2011). "The Aesthetics of Mythical Violence in Hong Kong Action Films." *New Cinema*, 8 (3), 155–67.

Vares, Tiina (2002). "Framing 'Killer Women' Films: Audience Uses of Genre." *Feminist Media Studies*, 2 (2), 213–29.

Filmography

Bigelow, Katherine (1995). *Strange Days*. U.S.

Bowman, Rob (2005). *Elektra*. U.S.

Bunuel, Luis, and Salvador Dali (1929). *The Andalusian Dog*. Fr.

——— (1930). *The Age of Gold*. Fr.

Cameron, James (1984). *The Terminator*. U.S.

——— (1986). *Aliens*. U.S.

——— (1991). *Terminator 2: Judgment Day*. U.S.

Caton-Jones, Michael (1995). *Rob Roy*. U.S.

Chow, Stephen (2005). *Kung Fu Hustle*. H.K.

Cosmatos, George (1985). *Rambo: First Blood Part II*. U.S.

Dahl, John (1994). *The Last Seduction*. U.S.

Eastwood, Clint (1992). *Unforgiven*. U.S.

Hawks, Howard (1938). *Bringing Up Baby*. U.S.

Hawks, Howard, and Richard Rosson (1932). *Scarface*. U.S.

Hogan, David (1996). *Barb Wire*. U.S.

Hu, King (1966). *Come Drink with Me*. H.K.

——— (1971). *Touch of Zen*. H.K.

Kloves, Steve (1989). *The Fabulous Baker Boys*. U.S.

Lee, Ang (2000). *Crouching Tiger, Hidden Dragon*. Taiwan, U.S., H.K., Ch.

McCarey, Leo (1937). *The Awful Truth*. U.S.
Morrison, Phil (2005). *Junebug*. U.S.
Noyce, Phillip (2010). *Salt*. U.S.
Peckinpah, Sam (1969). *The Wild Bunch*. U.S.
Penn, Arthur (1967). *Bonnie and Clyde*. U.S.
Scott, Ridley (1979). *Alien*. U.S.
——— (1991). *Thelma and Louise*. U.S.
Shichuan, Zhang (1926). *The Nameless Hero*. H.K.
Siu-Tung, Ching, and Stanley Tong (1992). *Swordsman II (The Legend of the Swordsman)*. H.K.
Tarantino, Quentin (2003–04). *Kill Bill (Volumes I and II)*. U.S.
——— (2012). *Django Unchained*. U.S.
To, Johnnie (1992). *The Heroic Trio*. H.K.
West, Simon (2001). *Lara Croft: Tomb Raider*. U.S.
Wilder, Billy (1944). *Double Indemnity*. U.S.
Wright, Joe (2011). *Hanna*. U.S. and Ger.
Yimou, Zhang (2004). *The House of Flying Daggers*. H.K. and China.
Yiu-leung, (Clarence) Fok (1992). *Naked Killer*. H.K.

3 Hyper-violence
The thrill of *Kill Bill*

Kill Bill is a revenge story and if we did not realize it on our own, Quentin Tarantino announces it in the epigram of the first installment of the tale (*Volume I*, 2003). The opening shot dramatizes the basis for the revenge. The character we will come to know as the "Bride" (Uma Thurman) lies bloodied and sobbing, in black and white. Feet walk toward her. A man talks and wipes her face tenderly with a handkerchief with the name "Bill" on it. The man denies behaving sadistically toward her. The Bride tells Bill (David Carradine) that the baby she is carrying is his and then a shot goes off. We never see Bill's face in *Volume I*, only hear the soothing cadences of his modulated voice.

I am treating this film as a paradigm of hyper-violence, even though the spectacle provided by hyper-violence is saved for the film's inventive and extended finale. In fact, by postponing the hyper-violence, serving it up only after a good deal of more commonplace cinematic destruction, Tarantino magnifies its impact. Tarantino not only presents all the ingredients that distinguish hyper-violence from its aesthetic counterparts, but he augments them with aesthetic inflections of lighting and rhythm. At the heart of hyper-violence is cinematic manipulation of the sensuous surface of human destruction in visually arresting ways. It resembles mega-violence insofar as its action is relatively realistic, as the feats of the characters are not extraordinary; they are not so beyond the reach of actual people as to require digital or photographic manipulation. Swinging a sword or throwing a knife the way the Bride and her enemies do could take place in the world outside the movie story.

However, the consequences of these actions, their drawn-out visual effects, could not be experienced in everyday life, as they require the artifice of the movie-maker. In this respect, hyper-violence is like surrealistic violence; however, in surrealistic violence the non-realistic dimension resides in the movements of the characters rather than in the aftermath of their violent action. The destructive consequences of hyper-violent action follow upon various amputations – the camera lingering over jets and plumes of blood. The slow-motion severing of an arm and the ensuing visual details of the gushing blood can only be produced by means of camera-work or film-editing. The aesthetic of such violence is found in the exaggeration and prolongation of the physical, human destruction. Hyper-violence intensifies the effects of bodily onslaught, for example, by enlarging upon the spatter of blood, enriching its color, and focusing on its pattern.

The film-story belongs to the Bride, who miraculously does not die as a result of the point blank shot to her head, taking revenge on three of Bill's henchwomen and, finally (in *Volume II*, 2004) on Bill himself. We learn this only after a relatively conventional, although bloody, fight between the Bride and Vernita Green (Vivica A. Fox) in a sunny California suburb. Although the battle is not sensational in the fashion of hyper-violence, it is important in establishing several gendered issues central to warrior women films that were discussed in the previous chapter. First is simply that the conflict in which the female action hero is caught up includes lethal combat with other women. Within this conflict, major tropes of film-stories that are driven by such women emerge: for example, the opposition between fighting prowess and femininity, including the denial of romantic love or family life to warrior women. Their expertise as killers appears to preclude the possibility of the joys long-associated with their gender. The tension between female violence and conventional female values/norms is thereby resolved by eliminating the conventional, leaving the fighting woman only her newly found formidable power.

Conventional skirmishing – a female feud

The film also explores a variety of relationships between the violent women and men. The Bride is most blatantly the antagonist of the title character, Bill (although not confronting him directly until the sequel); however, she will also need the help of another man: a master sword maker. In addition, Vernita is married (to an off-screen doctor, no less), and O-Ren Ishii (Lucy Liu) is the head of a band of chiefly male yakuza (Japanese mafia). Her dominant position is a reversal of Bill's command of his band of female assassins, for whom he functions as a seductive, pimp-lover boss. These themes and tropes involving questions of gender, power and life options give the film-story ballast. Some reviewers see the film chiefly in terms of stylistic mastery and flamboyance. Echoing other reviewers, such as Roger Ebert (2003), A. O. Scott describes Tarantino as "recklessly flaunting his formal skills as a choreographer of high-concept violence" (2003). Even though both critics praise the film, they overlook its deeper affinities with the intersecting gendered relationships that give many of the women warrior stories complexity and texture.

Other critics are quick to point out the sometimes annoying penchant Tarantino has for quoting or referencing other films. Among the numerous allusions to earlier kung fu films, for example, is an obvious homage to Bruce Lee (*Game of Death* 1972): the Bride's duplication of his yellow tracksuit. Because chronicling Tarantino's sometimes blatant, sometimes subtle referencing is peripheral to my interests, I will leave it to others to ferret them out or catalogue them.[1]

When a black woman, Vernita, answers the door of her sun-drenched, California home, we see a red-hued flashback of her doing violence to the Bride. The Bride immediately launches an attack that includes shattering glass, blood-letting and several kitchen implements and products. A humorous visual pun on feminine domesticity includes the Bride fending off a knife thrust with a skillet. The arrival of Vernita's adorable little daughter prompts the women to hide their knives. Although both combatants are bloodied and breathing hard, and the living room is in shambles, Vernita matter-of-factly asks her daughter, "How was school?" She then blames the disarray on the family dog, sends the girl to her room and offers the Bride coffee as if just catching up on old times, as she has indeed indicated to her little girl. The Bride assures Vernita, "I'm not going to murder you in front of your child," in a bow to the former assassin's new life. The Bride is obviously pained at Vernita's good fortune to have such a lovely child when hers has apparently been lost through the coma-inducing assault on her, and rejects Vernita's apology for "fucking her over." Vernita suggests a knife-fight that evening on the baseball diamond where she coaches Little League baseball. The un-gendered woman (deprived of child) versus flowering motherhood!

While ostensibly preparing cereal for her daughter, Vernita fires a concealed gun through the cereal box-violence hidden behind the props of parenthood. So much for mother's talk about sparing her daughter the violence. The Bride dodges the bullet, kicks a container of milk toward Vernita, and plunges a knife deep into her enemy's chest. By having Vernita renew the violence, the film positions the Bride as a "defensive" combatant, thereby inscribing the justificatory trope in female violence noted in the preceding chapter. Resuming the struggle in the supposed sanctuary of the kitchen, of course, risked exposing her daughter to the carnage, thereby diminishing the credibility of Vernita's transformation from killer to mother. After apologizing to the now motherless daughter, the Bride consults a notebook with a "death list five," and we realize that killing O-Ren has already occurred as her name has been crossed out. That episode will be told in flashback after another violent confrontation that resulted in the Bride driving a yellow pickup truck with "Pussy Wagon" written in big pink letters on the back.

After revealing that the Bride barely survived a massacre at her much earlier wedding site, the story shifts to the hospital in which she has lain comatose for four years. A tall blonde woman with an eye patch strolls down the corridor, dressed as a nurse, carrying a chemical-filled syringe. She is Elle Driver (Daryl Hannah), another member of the female assassination squad to which the Bride and Vernita once belonged. Elle is denied the pleasure of injecting the Bride with the lethal dose by a phone call from Bill who instructs her to stop, ostensibly to honor the Bride's toughness in surviving his wedding-day ambush. Again, we do not see Bill, just hear his velvety voice as his hand suggestively strokes the scabbard of an impressive sword. The Bride soon regains consciousness; remembering the moment she was shot and bemoaning the loss of the child she was carrying, she sobs.

The Bride lies down and hears a hospital orderly arranging a deal in what is obviously his ongoing, lucrative practice of selling the Bride for quasi-necrophiliac sex. Not only has a man (Bill) deprived the Bride of the feminine joy of having a child, but men have degraded her reproductive capacity with the help of another exploitative male. As the slobbering customer prepares to satisfy himself, the Bride enjoys a little impromptu revenge for the abuse she has unconsciously suffered. She bites him on the mouth and leaves him on the floor, unconscious or dead. The Bride soon has the returned orderly on the floor, bashes his head with the door, and takes his car keys – the keys to the "Pussy Wagon," now driven by one tough feline.

To prepare for her battle with O-Ren, The Bride travels to Okinawa to enlist the services of a renowned sword maker. She needs Hattori Hanzo to forge her a sword so charmed that its almost supernatural strength will enable her to vanquish an army of yakuza by destroying bodies and swords as easily as slicing bread. But first the Bride and Hattori engage in the sort of masquerade that is a staple of *House of Flying Daggers* (Zhang Yimou, 2004), one of our films that showcases surrealistic violence. Hattori plays the role of a simple shopkeeper to the Bride's culturally clumsy, western tourist. The Bride cuts the prosaic palaver off when she tells Hattori in fluent Japanese that she has come to see him, initiating their visit to his attic where the Bride admires his craftsmanship. Hattori informs the Bride that he is retired and keeps swords only for their aesthetic and sentimental value (a parallel with Tarantino, perhaps, who makes movies in the aesthetic traditions he loves). The Bride informs the master sword maker that she did not ask him to *sell* her a sword, but to *give* her one: apparently an important moral distinction in a warrior tradition such as the samurai. Hattori agrees to the Bride's request when she tells him that she needs the fabulous instrument to deal with a former student of his, implying that it is Bill. Hattori tells her she can sleep in the attic while he makes the sword, that she should practice and that he is going against an oath not to make weapons of death because he is sympathetic with her purpose. Once finished, Hattori proclaims it his finest sword, so we know it is in the realm of the mythic.

The climax of the first volume of *Kill Bill* is aptly labeled "Showdown at the House of Blue Leaves," and is dazzling in its hyper-violent ingenuity. The initial fight between the Bride and Vernita fits the bill of the classically plotted prologue to the main event: Westerns, samurai, boxing, and cops and robbers – the arc of the action moves toward the grand finale. The showdown will eventually feature the Bride against the icy O-Ren, but first she will have to dispatch the sadistic bodyguard and considerable army of O-Ren. O-Ren is currently the head of the Japanese underworld, but we had been told of her history and shown how she came to power, again in flashback.

O-Ren's history is also one of vengeance. Told in *anime* with the Bride narrating, O-Ren's parents are killed by a yakuza boss. O-Ren will later come to work for and then be backed in the Tokyo underworld by Bill, emerging as the head of the predominantly male gang; nevertheless, her relationships with men are as problematic as the Bride's. The night she takes complete control of the yakuza crime scene, her Chinese-Japanese American nationality is denigrated. Boss Tanaka challenges O-Ren's leadership of the yakuza council, calling it a perversion. O-Ren strides down the table top, beheads Tanaka, and a broad band of blood flies out of his neck. As the head rolls about, the film frame is filled with a crimson filigree, dancing in front of O-Ren's smiling, triumphant face.

The portrayal of the violence of O-Ren's ascendancy reinforces the preceding glimpse of hyper-violence. For no apparent reason other than sadistic delight, O-Ren's teenage bodyguard, Gogo Yubari (Chiaki Kuriyama), attacks a goofy, infatuated young man in a bar. She gleefully stabs him and a bucket of blood pours out of him, onto the floor. Even as the major confrontation between the Bride and O-Ren is foreshadowed by the Bride's lethal conflict with Vernita (another former colleague), so are we prepared for the hyper-violence of the showdown by the brief blood-letting of O-Ren and her protégé. As remarked in Chapter 1, a similar harbinger of all-out, hyper-violence orchestrates the action in *Django Unchained* (2012). In the latter, later cinematic offering by Tarantino, the crimson blood from a shot horseman that speckles fluffy white cotton balls on a sunny plantation anticipates an extended sequence of shadowy, no-holds-barred hyper-violence. The conventions of cinematic, narrative build-up give both films a familiar dramatic trajectory.

Hyper-violent climax

The hyper-violent finale of the film's periodic violence takes place inside a multi-level restaurant, and runs over twenty-five minutes. True to the incremental pacing of the violence noted above, the combat starts slowly, with the Bride engaged in single combat with a series of opponents. She begins by calling out O-Ren from below, on the restaurant's ground floor. The Bride is holding O-Ren's beautiful lieutenant (Sofie Fatale) "hostage," but soon slices off the woman's arm. From the now-disarmed shoulder, a fine mist of blood sprays as O-Ren's confederate writhes on the floor. The restaurant patrons wisely flee the advancing Bride attired in her yellow, blood-soaked jumpsuit. A parting shot of the lieutenant Sofie shows her on the ground, the last drops of blood flowing from her arm into a growing pool on the floor. The woman will somehow endure her maiming to carry the Bride's message of her victorious battle with O-Ren and her forces back to Bill.

One of O-Ren's male yakuza does a forward somersault off the balcony to confront the Bride. Her fabulous blade halves his sword, then plunges into him. The Bride lifts him into the air, skewered, then drops him into a decorative pool of water. O-Ren commands a brace of her men to "Tear the bitch apart." It is the same epithet hurled by Vernita at the Bride, denigrating her rival as female, but something less than a woman. The Bride quickly slays three men simultaneously, then a girl and another male. After taunting O-Ren with, "any more subordinates for me to kill?" the Bride is severely tested by the teenage bodyguard Gogo Yubari who is wielding a ball and chain.

Gogo comes down the stairs slowly and has a brief conversation with the Bride. The bodyguard girlishly giggles at the Bride's suggestion that she leave and swings the ball and chain like a lasso above her head. Gogo wraps the chain around the Bride's sword, yanks it from her and then knocks the Bride down with the ball. The Bride leaps backward, now holding a table leg as a weapon, and keeps jumping away, barely avoiding being hit by the lethal metal ball. Soon the ball, now sprouting blades, strikes and cuts the Bride's shoulder, after which Gogo coils the chain around the Bride's neck. Holding onto the chain for dear life, the Bride plunges the nailed end of the table leg into Gogo's foot, and then fling it into the girl's head, finishing her off.

Having barely survived the assault of O-Ren's precocious female bodyguard, the Bride must now do battle with a horde of O-Ren's male yakuza: the Crazy 88. Dozens of masked killers, formally attired in black, come storming into the restaurant from outside, streaking over railings and down the stairs. They fill the interior space, swords at the ready. An aerial shot shows the Bride completely surrounded by the yakuza. The full-scale display of hyper-violence is about to commence. Positioning the female O-Ren at the head of a gang of fighting men echoes the earlier *wuxia* film, *Naked Killer* (Fok Yiu-leung, 1992) in which "Princess and Baby hold sway over a small army of men who are completely cowed by their power" (Arons 2001: 36). Besides pitting women against one another, *Kill Bill* adds the dynamic of a woman attacking another female fighter (and former comrade) with an army of men, further marginalizing the possible claims of sisterhood. It is not enough for the Bride to struggle with Vernita and Gogo, but she must now defeat a more formidable female foe through the agency of her male minions.

As the Bride defends herself against the ensuing onslaught, masked faces are reflected in her mighty sword, as if presaging its imminent destination. Spinning and swinging her specially forged weapon, the Bride slices and dices her attackers with aplomb. Even as the male yakuza bleed, so is the sequence bled of color, replaced by stark black and white. Where black and white usually connotes cinematic realism, in *Kill Bill* it conduces to the unreality of hyper-violence. When a man's arm is severed, for example, the blood that spurts from the wound is rendered in a silvery spray. The Bride methodically flings hatchets intended for her into her assailants and stabs them with both forward and backward thrusts of her indestructible sword. The shimmering illumination of the Bride gives her a fairy-like aura, however gruesomely offset by the sounds of her opponents' vital fluids squishing, popping and gushing out of their bodies. When she chops off a man's head, mercury-toned blood geysers straight up from his gaping neck and from another yakuza yet more metallic blood fans out from his arm after it has been deftly freed of his hand. Translating the red of blood into the idiom of black and white not only provides aesthetic novelty, but it distances the audience from the unsavoriness of the carnage.

Although *Kill Bill* is energized by the hyper-violence toward which the more conventional battles have been building, it does offer a brief sample of the surrealistic violence that characterizes the *wuxia* movies I analyze in the following chapters. The Bride leaps on top of a man's shoulders and fights from the height as if mounted on a steed. She runs impossibly up the air onto the balcony, disposes of a few more of O-Ren's men, and after descending onto a table, cartwheels fantastically, slaying belligerents with athletic grace as she efficiently maneuvers her sword.

The color is restored, but when the restaurant's proprietress turns off the lights, the battling figures are illuminated in a blue light. The Bride now repulses her assailants in striking silhouette; she unleashes a grayish gout of blood by slashing off the arm of another masked combatant. With the lights back on, the Bride has two more opponents to vanquish before finally facing O-Ren herself. The first provides a moment of relative levity; he is a young man whose sword the Bride incrementally shortens, reducing it inch by inch with her blade, in obvious phallic allusion. She then spanks him with her weapon like a misbehaving boy, only to confront the final and most formidable yakuza on a narrow banister on the balcony. The man pirouettes several times in a display worthy of Fred Astaire, forcing the Bride to retreat. She ducks under a vicious blow and slices into his leg from which blood sluices. He plummets into the decorative pool below, deepening its mauve hue.

The Bride seeks out O-Ren through a door into a snowy, formal Japanese garden for the fight to the finish within the final showdown. As Todd McCarthy observes, "The climactic action settles down to a highly focused mano a mano . . . this fight, which is shot in carefully framed compositions, has the concentration and precision of a chess match" (2003). Slowing down the pace, of both action and camera-work, Tarantino ritualizes the last confrontations with "a tender elegance" (Peter Travers 2003). Clothed in a kimono that matches the snow, O-Ren asks where the Bride's impressive sword was made and unsheathes a gleaming weapon of her own. Suffering a deep gash to her back, The Bride goes down and appears to will herself upright (much as she willed her stiff limbs to move back in the hospital). O-Ren is also wounded: bent over, blood trickles down her sock and a line of her blood sparkles in the snow. Back in the fray, the Bride swings her sword and we see dark hair go flying. As O-Ren says, "That really was a Hattori sword," the camera pans to her face, revealing that the upper portion of her head has been lopped off along with the hair. For all the earlier bloodshed and gore, there is surprisingly little in the Bride's concluding triumph. O-Ren is spared the spumes and jets of blood that accompanied the demise of her soldiers. Although she loses a significant portion of her head, O'Ren's death feels measured and calm in marked contrast to the hectic, hyper-violence that has preceded it.

Of course, the drawn-out battle between the Bride and the army of O-Ren dazzles with the pyrotechnics of hyper-violence. But it is undergirded with meaning supplied by what has preceded it and the deliberate pace of the O-Ren denouement. After the frenetic and bloody hyper-violence, the unhurried duel between the Bride and O-Ren creates psychological space to gather the meaning that has been accumulating throughout the film-story. A good deal of that meaning concerns the themes we have seen clustered around the opposition between women as violent and women as caring. This opposition, in fact, is elaborated upon and further dramatized in the second installment of the Bride's story.

The film-story of *Volume I* is bookended by two fatal confrontations between a pair of woman warriors: the first bloody and vicious (in which the Bride kills Vernita), the second civilized and calm, in which the Bride outduels O-Ren. Although the Bride has had to kill dozens of men in between, the revenge she takes on two of her former female comrades feels paramount. It seems to speak to the loss of sisterhood, perhaps because the female alliance was, after all, controlled by a man – Bill. But all is not quite as it has seemed for the Bride, for Bill asks the miraculously surviving lieutenant, Sofie, whether the Bride is aware that the female child she was carrying is still alive.

Backstory: women cannot have it all

The little girl who survived, and the Bride's discovery of her latent moth-erhood, are the crux of the second part of the Bride's saga: *Kill Bill Volume II* (2004). There is no hyper-violence in the second film and precious little mayhem even of the old-fashioned variety. The Bride's knock-down, drag-out scrimmage with (the one-eyed) Elle is the centerpiece of the film's violence. Having fought a black woman (Vernita) and an Asian woman (O-Ren) in Volume I, the Bride completes her female combat with a mirror image: a blonde, blue-eyed assassin. Despite punching, kicking, cutting and hurling, the Bride defeats Elle by ripping out her remaining eye (and then squashing it under foot). She does not directly kill her, but leaves the trailer in which they fought with the sightless Elle screaming and writhing. Elle may be fatally killed (off-screen) by the snake that she had planted to kill Budd in a preceding scene.

Although Budd had been on the Bride's original revenge list, that confrontation is abbreviated when Budd buries the Bride alive after efficiently shooting her with salt rock. We are shown her demanding training with the master Pai Mei (Gordon Liu), in yet another temporal switchback, by way of explaining how she is able to punch her way out of her coffin, emerging for a second time from a near-death state. Where earlier, the Bride surfaces from a long coma into consciousness and story, now the heroine physically pulls herself out of the earth, into life-giving air. The ultimate battle, with Bill, is anti-climactic from the standpoint of a skillful or visually entertaining violent conflict. Its value lies in the exposition that helps makes sense of the massacre at the wedding chapel: what led up to it and why Bill orchestrated it.

When the Bride (whom we have learned is named Beatrix Kiddo) enters Bill's Mexican hacienda, she is stunned to discover her own beautiful 5-year-old daughter, who unhesitatingly calls her "mommy." In a warm, paternal style, Bill has the child, B.B., play at shooting and being shot by her mother. After putting her daughter to bed, having viewed the video "Shogun Assassin," Bea is forced to explain to Bill why she ran away from him, pregnant with his child. The explanation reinforces and deepens the trope that has become the cornerstone of the narrative in many female-centered martial arts films: that excelling in the techniques of violence is incompatible with a fulfilling romantic or domestic life. Vernita's golden, suburban idyll with a successful husband and lovely daughter, for example, is sabotaged when the Bride resurrects Vernita's bloody past. The finale reprises Vernita's domesticity, with Bea and B.B. replacing Vernita and her little girl.

The explanation for Bea's flight from Bill turns on her discovery of her pregnancy during an assignment from Bill to kill a woman named Lisa

Wong. In the midst of fending off another female assassin, sent by the would-be victim Lisa Wong to kill her, Bea cites her pregnancy to call off the shoot-out. Bea persuades her Asian counterpart to quit the fight on the basis of her imminent motherhood. The erstwhile counter-assassin humorously says, "Congratulations," before leaving the battle scene in a hotel. The Asian killer sympathizes with Bea's desire for motherhood and perhaps also with her maternal aversion to the ways of violence. The suggestion seems to be that virtually all women warriors harbor the more traditional feelings and desires involved in womanhood – or at least respect such feelings and desires.

Bea tells Bill that once the pregnancy kit "strip turned blue" she could not kill for him anymore (perhaps, especially kill women). She had been his woman, Bea says, but had chosen her daughter over Bill and his world. She wanted her daughter to be free of Bill's influence, to have a "clean slate." At the very least, on Bea's understanding, the flight from Bill is also an escape from violence to loving motherhood. The two are incompatible. Bill's assault at the chapel, then, is also vengeful. Bea had not only failed to carry out her assassin's assignment, but she had disappeared from Bill's life: intolerable for someone who has to be in control. Bea's survival, first of the coma resulting from Bill shooting her in the head, and then from being buried alive, is fueled by the lust for revenge as well. The fact that the terminus of her journey of revenge is a darling daughter may make Bea's future motherhood seem a bit problematic. Can she succeed in shedding her old violent life, like a snakeskin, and live happily ever after with B.B. (the initials of her parents, Bill and Bea?) where Vernita could not?

After Bea's account of why she deserted him, Bill suggests a swordfight on the adjoining beach at midnight. The suggestion echoes Vernita's offer of a night fight on a neighboring ballfield. And as with Vernita, the violence breaks out sooner, indoors, in a home. The "duel" is terribly anti-climactic, leaving the audience to wonder whether Tarantino has simply exhausted his store of movie mayhem magic. He does not even try to present an interesting, much less demanding, tableau of violence. Instead, we see a few quick, closely shot sword thrusts and parries, mostly while the couple is seated. Then Bea delivers the famed Five Point Palm Exploding Heart Technique that the master Pai Mei had indeed taught her, but not Bill. Bea is tearful as she strokes Bill's hand and tells him he is ready – to take the few steps legend has it that precede the inevitable death from the fatal technique.

The film-story concludes with Bea and B.B. hugging and smiling. The apparent resolution of the tension between the life of violence and domesticity for women warriors is simply posited in an image: the violence is to give way to a loving relationship. With the death of Bill and the others on Bea's hit list, perhaps she will be free to change. Given the way learning of her pregnancy ignited her rejection of her former life, Bea does seem to have a strong impulse to devote herself to her daughter. Lisa Purse interprets the finale as establishing Bea's motherhood as a way of "containing" her flair for violence (2011: 85). Motherhood complements the film's other domestic positioning of Bea: her being "groomed for action by an influential father figure" – Bill himself and perhaps the Master Pei as well (84). In the preceding chapter, I discussed how domesticating the action heroine is among various cinematic strategies to blunt or mitigate her physical power and thereby make her less threatening. Exaggerating her sexuality is another, as it, too, places the strong woman in a familiar social space, one that men especially find appealing.

On the other hand, Bea has a long history of killing and has told Bill in their final conversation that she did enjoy eliminating her enemies. The violent work is satisfying. The future of Bea and B.B. may after all depend on the accuracy of Bill's declaration to Bea that she is a "natural born killer." Like Superman, he says, her nature was determined from her birth and the ordinary trappings of daily life, like Clark Kent's pedestrian attire, merely cover up her extraordinary powers.[2] If Bill is correct, then Bea will find it difficult, perhaps impossible, to supplant the thrill of violence with the quiet satisfactions of motherhood. I am less convinced that Bea will be able to transition from soldier to mother than Purse seems to be. I find the story's conclusion open-ended, shadowed by the failure of Vernita to live happily ever after with her equally charming daughter, in sun-drenched California. The closing shot seems to me to be more interrogative, asking whether the woman warrior can coexist with or grow into a nurturing, traditional female.

Notes

1 Peter Hitchcock also takes issue with Tarantino's infatuation with "elliptical scrambling of events sequences," another stylistic feature that I note but do not dwell upon (2007: 227).
2 Tarantino uses the occasion to have Bill insert an interesting aside with regard to other superheroes. Other superheroes, from Spiderman to Batman, adorn themselves in costumes to function heroically; only Superman dons costume to conceal his heroic stature.

Bibliography

Arons, Wendy (2001). "'If Her Stunning Beauty Doesn't Bring You to Your Knees, Her Deadly Drop Kick Will': Violent Women in the Hong Kong Kung Fu Film." *Reel Knockouts: Violent Women in the Movies*, Eds. M. McCaughey and N. King, pp. 27–51. Austin, TX: University of Texas Press.
Ebert, Roger (2003). "*Kill Bill*." *RogerEbert.com*, Oct. 10, 2003, Reviews.

Hitchcock, Peter (2007). "Niche Cinema, or 'Kill Bill with Shaolin Soccer'." *Hong Kong Film, Hollywood and the New Global Cinema: No Film Is an Island*, Eds. G. Marchetti and T. See Kam, pp. 219–32. New York: Routledge.

McCarthy, Todd (2003). "*Kill Bill.*" *Variety*, Sept. 30.

Purse, Lisa (2011). *Contemporary Action Cinema*. Edinburgh: Edinburgh University Press.

Scott, A.O. (2003). "Film Review: Blood Bath and Beyond." *New York Times Online*, Oct. 10, 2003.

Travers, Peter (2003). "*Kill Bill Vol. 1.*" *Rolling Stone*, Oct. 9. rollingstone.com/movies/reviews/kill-bill-vol.-1-20031009.

Filmography

Lee, Bruce (1972). *The Game of Death*. H.K.

Tarantino, Quentin (2003). *Kill Bill (Volume I)*. U.S.

——— (2004). *Kill Bill (Volume II)*. U.S.

——— (2012). *Django Unchained*. U.S.

Yimou, Zhang (2004). *House of Flying Daggers*. H.K. and China.

Yiu-leung, (Clarence) Fok (1992). *Naked Killer*. H.K.

4 Surrealistic violence

No muscles, no splatter

Surrealistically portrayed cinematic violence distances the aestheticization of violence still further from realistic and mega-violence. As with hyper-violence, the surrealistic variety is obviously fashioned by means of film digitization; however, dismemberment and blood-letting are transcended by magical action. For this reason, the action in these films is sometimes referred to as "fantasist" or "fantasy" (Arons 2001: 27–51). I will discuss the surrealistic violence in two *wuxia* films that seem to me to be paradigms of this subgenre: *Crouching Tiger, Hidden Dragon* (Ang Lee, 2000) and *The House of Flying Daggers* (Zhang Yimou, 2004). Graceful, unworldly movement of the human body and costume predominate in both. To this, the second film adds surrealistic violence of weaponry. These emblematic Asian films exhibit cinemagraphic creativity in lifting violence off the ground and into an almost ethereal realm of beauty (choreographed by Yuen Wo-ping and Tony Ching Siu-tung, respectively).

Defying gravity, the combatants spin and wheel in the air, attacking and evading; they carom off buildings and spring from the limbs of trees, sometimes wielding swords, sometimes using hands, arms and legs to assault or parry. Through the manipulations of digitized photographic technology as well as wire work, characters float, swoop and soar in hypnotically enchanting choreography. The films transport the audience to a weightless realm of motion conjured out of acrobatic inventiveness and the spirit of play. It is as if the centrality of women infused the traditional martial arts story with dance to create a dreamscape.

Conflicted women in combat

The surrealistic films are distinguished by their emphasis on the behavior and interests of women. The hyper-violence of the *Kill Bill* (Quentin Tarantino, 2003, 2004) movies is certainly inscribed in the plot and plight of its female warriors, most conspicuously those of their hero, the Bride. However the stories told in the films defined by surrealistic violence develop and extend themes of gender in far-reaching and provocative ways. In particular, the films of surrealistic violence raise questions of social and political import; where *Kill Bill* involved a gang of female assassins under the control of the eponymous male ringleader, *Crouching Tiger, Hidden Dragon* and *House of Flying Daggers* focus upon women who are either excluded from the ranks of the martial arts or are oppressed by the prevailing, masculine military-political establishment. In both cases, the relationship of women to violence is framed in existential terms: the choices and paths to fulfillment of the central female characters are essentially connected to battle.

In these film-stories, the embrace by women of martial arts is at once symptom and cause of their gendered conflict. Women express the social and psychological tensions that beset them by having recourse to combat; moreover, some of their dissatisfaction arises from being excluded from the battlefield of the martial arts. The forceful, rapid-fire blows of Bruce Lee give way to the elegant leaps and somersaults of the captivating Zhang Ziyi – the female star of both films discussed here. Consonant with their feminine orientation, the films replace impressive male musculature with the fine-boned beauty of women in silken garb. Although Zhang Ziyi is stunning, she does not project sexuality so much as disaffected elegance.

The story of *Crouching Tiger, Hidden Dragon* revolves about the competition for the soul of a winsome, spirited young woman who is an aristocrat but wishes to live the life of a woman warrior. The four people who vie to direct the future of Jen Wu (Zhang Ziyi) can be paired according to whether they operate within the conventional norms that govern their society. First is a mature couple famed for their fighting skills who endeavors to take Jen under their wing. Li Mu Bai (Chow Yun-fat) and his unconsummated love, Yu Shu Lien (Michelle Yeoh), try to steer the impetuous girl in what they view as the right direction. Li is retiring from the life of combat but, intrigued by the obvious talent of Jen, wishes to make her his disciple. He represents the legitimate study of the classical martial arts taught to the elite at Wudan Mountain.[1] His female comrade, Shu, is an advocate for traditional marriage. She explicitly speaks of Jen's impending marriage favorably, something she clearly has wanted with Li for quite some time, and she repeatedly pulls Jen back to earth, from her airy flights during their first skirmish. Shu's attempts to render Jen earthbound, when the girl wishes to soar, fit nicely with the older woman's tradition-bound view of happiness as lying within the boundaries of conventional marriage. Shu most fully exemplifies L.S. Kim's view that the female Asian action hero does not challenge the powerful patriarchal structure, as she is "simultaneously heroic and traditional" (2006). On the other hand, Jen and her governess do defy patriarchal strictures.

A counterpoint to the traditions embodied in the fighting duo of Li and Shu is the possibility of rebellious happiness held out by Jade Fox (Pei-pei Cheng) and Lo (Chang Chen). Jen has been surreptitiously trained in the martial ways of Wudan Mountain by her governess, the scheming rebel, Jade Fox, who had been denied acceptance to the nonpareil school because of her gender. Teaching her lady how to fight, Jade hopes to team with Jen as warrior outlaws. Lo also represents a life that rejects the norms of proper society, as he is a desert bandit whose love for Jen (revealed in a flashback) is reciprocated by her.[2] Jen could choose to live with him on the margins of the conventional norms that regulate the behavior of women in her culture. This would seem the most appealing alternative. Staying with Lo would allow Jen to follow the path of a woman warrior with a romantic companion instead of caving in to her aristocratic family's wish that she live the staid life of the wife of a well-placed nobleman with whom she is not in love.

The fact that in *Crouching Tiger, Hidden Dragon* all the physical conflict involves women, often pitted against one another, emblematizes the prominence of women in the surrealistic subgenre of action movies. In addition, the exclusion of women from heroic work is essential to the plot. Jade Fox has killed the revered teacher of Wudan Mountain because she was not allowed to study the martial arts under him. She subsequently pilfered the training manual, using it to teach Jen the mysteries hitherto reserved exclusively for male students. Then, too, Jen pines for the excitement and freedom of a warrior's life rather than tread the well-worn path of a lord's wife. L.S. Kim sees these women along with Shu Lien as representing a "societal struggle brought upon them because of (*sic*) they reached beyond more appropriate gender roles" (2006).

The two most complex relationships that Jen has are with the other women, Jade Fox and Shu, not the men. In both cases, affection and attraction are mingled with hostility. It seems as though women warriors have more tensions to resolve between themselves because of their new roles and ambitions. Although Jade has helped Jen become proficient in the martial arts, the girl has since surpassed her teacher. Where the lower class and illiterate Jade could only work with the images in the manual from Wudan Mountain, Jen was able to read the text and did not help Jade expand her own powers. When Jade learns of Jen's withholding knowledge, therefore, she becomes resentful and wishes to destroy her erstwhile protégé. On the other hand, despite professing a desire for sisterhood with Shu, Jen balks at the more experienced woman's attempt to influence her. As a result, the most extended and varied combat takes place between Jen and Shu toward the movie's end.

While the plot is driven by the pursuit of Jen by these four seasoned fighters, the central object of interest (what Hitchcock might have called

the "McGuffin") is the majestic sword "Green Destiny," an obvious fore-
runner of the Bride's special sword in *Kill Bill*.[3] In relinquishing his life
as a practitioner of the martial arts, Li asks Shu to deposit the sword with
their friend and protector, Sir Te, in Peking. In Te's home, Shu meets Jen
and shows her the 400-year-old sword. They talk and Jen reveals her desire
to have the freedom of a fighter. Jen has a distorted vision of a swordsman, gleaned from books, as living impulsively, without restrictions. Jen
imagines an uncaged life where she can "roam around free." It is a conception of freedom as license: doing what one wishes without being limited by
outside pressures or norms. However crudely expressed by Jen, the theme
of freedom is understood by her as an attractive alternative to conventional
marriage and its bondage. Jen does not see other options for herself, but
Shu cautions her. She points out that the life of the warrior is informed by
rules, rules that govern friendship, trust and integrity. Without rules there
is no survival. The exchange between Jen and Shu actually contains three
conceptions of the good life: conventional marriage; untrammeled action
and battle; noble battle with a code of honor.

Although he sees Jen as a female knight-errant, Stephen Teo nevertheless interprets her "as an ambivalent character, and this departs from the
heroic tradition in the *wuxia* movie" (2005: 200). Jen's capricious attitude
and unwillingness to take instruction from either Shu or Li indicate, for Teo,
a failure of character. Jen's attraction to Shu, yet rebellion against her, for
example, demonstrate a lack of moral compass, prompting her to act almost
exclusively on whim. As Teo argues, "Jen shows by her behavior that she
lacks the moral standards of a true knight-errant" (201). L.S. Kim concurs,
citing Jen's disrespectful conduct as evidence that "she demonstrates a lack
of understanding of the warrior (*giang hu*) code of ethics" (2006). Jen's
moral flaw, the shakiness of her moral moorings, could be part of an explanation of her inability to reconcile the life of a warrior woman with lasting
friendship or love.

It is significant that the first and, later, the most elaborate and extended
battle are between the two women who oscillate between friendship and
enmity. They are complex individuals and find in one another qualities that
attract and also repel. As a result, their relationship is the most interesting and
perhaps the most revealing with regard to the challenges faced by women
warriors. In the first skirmish of the film, Shu Lien pursues the masked thief
of the legendary sword (Jen, of course). After easily dispensing with male
guards, Jen must contend with the combat-tested, older woman. Roger Ebert
admires the "sheer physical grace" of the sequence: "As the characters run
up the sides of walls and leap impossibly from one house to another. . . .
It is done so lightly, quickly, easily" (Ebert 2000). Shu dogs the girl over
tiled rooftops, matching her impossible aerial bursts. Much of the fighting

and fleeing occur across this roofscape of tan, textured tiles. The abstract design of the context augments the artistic, fantastic dynamic of the scene. The lighting enhances the rooftop aesthetic to create "a fight of incredible strangeness, stark moonlit mystery – and delirious excitement" (Bradshaw 2001: 1).

To reach Jen, Shu caroms upward, between walls, as if climbing a steep, uneven, giant staircase. Jen runs on and through the air, on rooftops, bounding from Shu. After some standard hand-to-hand kung fu fighting, Jen flies up to the roof and Shu scampers up a wall to resume the battle. There is more hand-to-hand and foot-to-foot fighting: quickly struck blows and swirling kicks. Against the rhythm of a crisp drumbeat, the spinning and twirling of the struggle is itself beautiful, surprisingly purged of the blatant straining and suffering of male-centered or killer women martial arts films. In the midst of one of their moments of hand fighting, Shu orders the thief to give back the sword. Jen runs to a wall, pushes off from it, and projects herself, parallel to the ground, at her adversary. Shu repulses her. A quick overhead shot presents the pair spinning kicks rapid-fire at each other, perfectly synchronized. In the next, basic side shot, Jen and Shu are leaping and kicking, still in a precise dance. Shu pulls a hair stick from the thief, confirming her suspicions that it is Jen who has taken the sword. Jen finally flees for good by pushing off a wall and soaring through the air, again parallel to the ground, sprinting up a building, and alighting from the roof into the night sky.

A repeated trope adds meaning to the pure aesthetic of the surrealistic violence: the trope of flight-aspiration. The youthful Jen keeps trying to escape upward, into the air. The more conventional woman, Shu, keeps pulling the girl down, to ground. The repetition of this image inscribes competing perspectives on the physical conflict between the two women. Jen's repeated attempts to flee into the air suggest the aspirations that she has confided to Shu: freedom from the social and political constraints that act like gravity, weighing her down. The martial arts taught at Wudan Mountain seem to Jen the path away from a fettered and smothering domestic future. She resents the fact that the family of her fiancé will be good for her father's career. She desires "to be free to choose [her own life], to choose whom I love."

On the other hand, Shu represents tradition and conventional routes of fulfillment. For all her expertise in combat, Shu yearns for marital union with Li and will later advise Jen to make a similar choice. The tension for women warriors between a life of combat and one of a loving relationship that I analyzed earlier (in Chapters 2 and 3), seems crystallized in Shu. The resolution she would prefer is to give up fighting and settle down with the man she has long loved – an option that Vernita in *Kill Bill* sought but proved short-lived. Shu is denied her vision of happiness because Li is killed toward the end of the film-story; moreover, he is done in by the machinations of another female fighter – the devious Jade Fox. The thwarting of Shu's notion of a good life keeps the opposition between war and (domestic) peace very much in the forefront of the saga of the warrior queen.

Yet as the story unfolds, we learn that the notorious Jade Fox is not as straightforwardly evil as may at first seem to be the case. Before stealing the secret martial arts manual from Wudan Mountain, she poisoned the martial arts master, even as she will poison Li toward story's end. *Kill Bill* also mimics, or pays homage, to Jade's murderous ways by having Elle poison the imposing martial arts master Pai Mei, who taught the Bride how to fence, break boards with her hands and deliver the famed "Five Point Palm Exploding Heart" blow. Nevertheless, Jade Fox has grounds for hostility. The master was quite happy to have (unwed) sex with her, but refused to share with her his profound knowledge of the martial arts. In addition, she is illiterate due to her lower class. Although she is diabolical – killing the Wudan master and Li, and planning to do in her once beloved Jen – Jade represents the woman of action whose ambition and passion have been perverted by the social obstacles that her gender and class entail. Even as Shu had envisioned a tranquil life with a retired Li, Jade had pictured an exciting life of violence teamed up with Jen: an all-female couple. Jade counsels Jen to run away with her instead of wasting her life "as the wife of some bureaucrat."

Jade herself is involved in a brief stint of surrealistic violence. As she fights off a trio of combatants, Li intervenes. In the moonlight, Jade performs a stunning cartwheel in response to Li's threatening advances. Just as Li is about to avenge his master's death by killing Jade, Jen appears. She leaps and executes a backward somersault in attacking Li. Soon, she and Jade escape into the air. In a following scene, Li offers to be Jen's teacher of the martial arts. He says that she has potential but, although studying the Wudan manual, she does not really understand it. Jen spurns his offer and, once again, takes off into darkened air. Li soon contends with Shu about Jen's future, telling her that the girl needs direction and training. Shu notes that Jen is an aristocrat, unlike them, and thinks the situation is best resolved by Li killing Jade Fox and Jen getting married, as arranged by her parents. Li disagrees, proposing that Jen come to Wudan to be a (non-traditional, because female) disciple, otherwise she would become an outlaw, a "poisoned dragon." Discipleship to Li offers a middle way for Jen. It lies between the traditional marriage, advocated and desired by Shu, and the outlaw life of martial arts adventure offered by Jade. Li's suggestion would contain the martial arts adventure within the structure, tradition and legitimacy of the Wudan school. The film-story prods us to favor this compromise for the talented and attractive but headstrong Jen.

If she could also have a meaningful romantic relationship, why so much the better!

Warrior women and romance

A flashback provides an interlude in the arc of the story during which Jen had seemed to find an alternative middle way: a combination of outlaw martial arts and romantic affection. It is occasioned by the arrival of Lo in Jen's chamber in Peking, in the story's present. Lo wants Jen to return with him to the desert where they could continue Lo's marauding ways and enjoy their passionate relationship. I construe the desert as a place symbolically removed from the cultural norms that constrain Jen and Lo. Following Stanley Cavell's interpretation of forests in Shakespearean comedy and countryside in many of the remarriage comedies of Hollywood, the desert functions as a realm apart: "a place in which perspective and renewal are to be achieved" (Cavell 1981: 49).[4] The shift in perspective and renewal of spirit are especially keen for individuals involved in romantic relationships or poised to become so entangled. Although neither a Shakespearean nor a Hollywood comedy, *Crouching Tiger, Hidden Dragon* resonates with these humorous romances by situating lovers in a place that harbors them from the routines and expectations of their usual civilized environs. And not only for Jen and Lo.

A parallel interaction soon occurs between Li and Shu, whose romantic attraction had long simmered beneath the surface of their camaraderie. Sitting at a table in a secluded wood, Li puts his hand over Shu's and places her hand next to his face. Li confesses that he's never had the courage to touch her hand before, ironic given his surpassing martial courage. Li says he wants to be with her, "like this," in the peaceful forest. The implication is that, as with Jen and Lo in the desert, Li and Shu would have to eschew the complexities of city life, such as found in bustling Peking, in order to transform their lives from one of battle to domestic tranquility. The desire for and partial attainment of a romantic liaison distinguishes the Asian female fighter from most of her American counterparts. As L.S. Kim observes, "Unlike earlier attempts in U.S. films to establish women action heroes – *Terminator 2, G.I. Jane, Alien* – these Asian women do not have to become men or asexual in order to take up the role of hero" (2006).[5]

In a flashback to some time before the film-story takes place, Lo and his horsemen raid the well-appointed caravan in which Jen is traveling. Reaching into the coach, Lo plucks an ivory comb from Jen's hair and playfully winks at her. Jen soon hops on a horse and rides after the dashing bandit. They tussle on horseback; Jen is knocked to the ground and defies Lo's advice that she return to her mother. In fits and starts, Jen continues after Lo, fighting and resting for water (provided by Lo), and wrestling in the sand. Jen awakens from a blow in a nicely furnished desert cave in which Lo is inexplicably alone, without his band of horsemen.

Christina Klein cites the connotations of the fight between Jen and Lo as an example of how Ang Lee departs from typical martial arts films by integrating the exhilarating spectacle of fight scenes with the film's narrative. In *Crouching Tiger, Hidden Dragon*, the high octane battles no longer interrupt narrative flow, but "worked to progress the story, develop the characters, and express the themes" (Klein 2004: 32). The tussle between the attractive young people isolated from other individuals vibrates with eroticism: "Jen and Lo's vigorous fight in the desert communicates their sexual attraction as well as their shared social defiance" (34). Klein supports her claim about the integration of the combat spectacle with narrative with other examples, including the fact that the first fight scene in the movie does not occur right away (as is typical in most martial arts films), but only after characters and story-line have been established. Those characters and story-line include the suppressed love that Shu and Li have felt for each other over a long period of time.

Not all critics share Klein's enthusiasm for the film's considerable attention to romantic involvement. Stephen Teo finds that the romantic, non-action scenes have a dampening effect on the "intoxicating choreography" (2000). I think that he overlooks two ways in which the romantic dimension works with the vibrancy of combat. First, as Klein suggests, the erotic charge of Jen's strenuous fights with Lo braid together romance with close fighting. Second, when the two couples calmly talk, those scenes provide a substantive, narrative balance to the physical conflict, informing the movie with a rhythmic undertone. Peter Bradshaw praises director Lee for giving the relationship between the mature and youthful couples a pivotal role in the unfolding of the fight-filled plot: "Ang Lee's achievement is to reconnect the genre [*wuxia* within 'magic realism'] with its innate, latent sense of decorum and romance, qualities which have been ignored or treated ironically or unintelligently" (2001: 1).

Teo also takes issue with the way in which the film fails to live up to the tradition of heroism in martial arts literature and cinema. The romantic relationships in the film "water down" the heroic dimension and none of the characters adequately realizes the stature of the hero or makes unequivocally noble choices. For Teo, the essence of martial arts stories is "the heroic principle as the tragic manifestation of chivalric violence" (2000). It includes, or necessitates, clear choices for the hero and simple distinctions between good and evil. However, I would argue that the complexities of *Crouching Tiger, Hidden Dragon* add to its depth. Ang Lee further complicates the standard, clean line of *wuxia* stories with such non-romantic elements as Jade Fox's exclusion from the teaching at Wudan Mountain and the conflicted feelings between Jen and Shu. My disagreement with Teo could, of course, be due to my Western approach to narrative, favoring as it does the complexity of layered meaning and conflicted character.[6]

Jen has pursued Lo, ostensibly to retrieve her cherished ivory comb. It seems to be an intimate counterpoint to the sword of Green Destiny as an emblematic object or talisman. What it symbolizes is unclear. Perhaps in Jen's hands it symbolizes luxurious, aristocratic life married to a boring bureaucrat (in the words of Jade Fox). In Lo's hands, the comb may hold the promise of a daring nomadic life, free of the social mores that Jen finds oppressive. In any event, it will reappear during Lo's nocturnal visit to Jen in the present action of the film-story. In the flashback, Jen is in Lo's desert cave once again. Having knocked Lo out and wandered dangerously in the desert, she has been rescued by the bandit. He provides the girl with some precious water for a bath and removes himself. Lo charmingly tells Jen that he will sing from outside the cave so she can be assured of privacy. After her bath, Jen tells Lo that she has come only for the comb he has filched from her, and their renewed wrestling turns to lovemaking. She nestles against the desert rogue and, for the first time in the film-story, seems content.

Ironically, it is Lo who sends Jen back to her family and conventional society. The couple is now up in the mountains, trying to elude the search party that Jen's father has sent out. Lo tells Jen that the men are trouble for him and suggests that she return to her parents and that he will earn their respect. Before they part, Jen gives him the comb he had returned, saying that he can give it back, again, when they reunite – which we see taking place as it occurs, in the story's present. Lo visits Jen in Peking and tells her that he has come to stop her marriage. But when Jen sends him away, Lo once more relinquishes the special comb. In Jen's hands, once again, the comb now seems to symbolize a rejection of the middle way of a martial arts life with a lover outside the bounds of social norms. Whether it indicates the girl's willingness to settle down in a stodgy marriage, however, remains to be seen. With Li's letter of introduction, Lo will go to Wudan Mountain, eventually to await Jen.

A talented woman triumphant

One of the most inventive scenes of surrealistic high-jinks takes place in the interior of a bustling restaurant. Disdainful of a band of male bullies, Jen goads them into a lop-sided brawl. Deficient in the more refined techniques of combat, the men are little more than props by means of which Jen can display her remarkable acrobatics and surrealistic terpsichore. "She takes on and defeats a host of men . . . in the kind of inn scene made famous in King

Hu movies, uttering comic one liners as she overcomes each opponent" (O'Day 2004: 212). The thugs tend to be thick and bulky, accentuating the girl's lithe agility. After gently alighting on a banister, Jen glides from one railing to another, then onto the floor of the restaurant's second story. She performs a series of backflips down the stairs, only to run over the top of the man following her down the stairs. After a dazzling back somersault, the be-robed Jen ascends through the air in a long vertical spin, looking like a high-speed augur, back to the second level of the building. She wields the stolen sword quickly and efficiently, but sheds no blood and kills no one. She then reverses her earlier gymnastic routine by descending to the first floor in a dive with a triple, front somersault. Jen propels herself like a missile out of the restaurant, fights with her sword, then floats up into the building to strike and hold an arresting sword-fighting pose.

Christina Klein explains how the reconfiguration of the physical space of the inn enhances the depiction of the fighting, especially Jen's surrealistic whimsy.

> Over the course of the fight, this space is redefined as tables are smashed, walls are crashed through, and banisters collapse. Virtually all the physical boundaries that demarcate the internal tavern spaces . . . are penetrated. . . . The fight does not so much take place *within* (sic) a physical space, as the physical space becomes an element that the fighters incorporate into their fight and that they transform in the process.
>
> (2004: 30)

A minor cut on an adversary's lip is the only trace of blood during the altercation, its isolated occurrence subtly indicating the surrealistic abandonment of old-fashioned brutality. We rarely, if ever, see the gruesome effects of a well-timed blow or well-placed kick. Although after the mayhem the assembled louts are portrayed as banged, bruised, and bandaged, they seem comical as they complain to Li and Shu of their drubbing at the hands of the evasive Jen. For despite the snicker-snack of her sword, Jen has unleashed no gouts of blood, severed no limbs, and slain no adversary. True, several people die in the course of the film-story. Jade Fox kills the policeman who hunts her for murder with a spinning blade and her poison darts end both her own and Li's lives. But we never see mortal blows delivered either through martial arts wizardry or swordplay. Surrealistic violence itself is untainted by gore or its fatal aftermath. In elevating the magical fighting to choreographed, often mid-air movement, surrealistic violence also tends to displace the shocking, albeit alluring, bloody impact of more realistic and hyper-violence.

Ambivalence and battle

At Shu Lien's headquarters, Jen shows up, repeating her wish for a sisterly relationship. Holding a tearful Jen, Shu admonishes the girl for causing much trouble. Shu again expresses her traditional attitude, saying "You can run from marriage, but not your parents." She advises Jen to return to her parents and then decide about Lo. Shu suggests accompanying Jen to Peking and helping her find a solution to her difficulties. But when Shu mentions that Li has sent Lo to Wudan Mountain, Jen is upset. She sees Li's action as manipulative and somehow "setting her up." After a heated exchange between the two women, they engage in a long battle during which Shu avails herself of a variety of weapons.

Describing the courtyard in Shu's compound and how the fight is photographed within it, Klein draws out implications for meaning and composition. The courtyard is

> a rectilinear open space whose rectilinear shape is reinforced by the worn stone floor and the vertically placed boards of the unfinished wooden walls. . . . This simple staging [by choreographer Yuen Wo-ping] immediately establishes this is a contest between two equally skilled opponents and puts the visual emphasis on the movements of the fighters – and on their weapons.
>
> (2004: 29)

Shu responds to Jen's Green Destiny with a machete. After a sword clinch, Jen eludes Shu with spinning gyrations parallel to the floor. She then catapults herself off a wall to attack Shu who herself performs a gravity-reduced, airborne diagonal pirouette out of harm's reach. Shu then fights with a long, metal-tipped wooden pole. Pinned with her back on a table, Jen executes another spinning aerial evasion as Shu slashes with the blade of her implement. Shu next comes at Jen with a pair of blades that are equipped with handles and curved ends, like small lethal staffs, that can be swung separately or hooked together. As if that were not enough, Shu proceeds to seize a metal pike and hurl it at Jen. Shu smacks Jen's sword with another metal pike and the girl retreats by briefly floating backwards. Finally, Jen cuts the implement in half with the fabled sword. As Shu advances on Jen with another powerful-looking sword, Jen runs up a wall and backflips over Shu. Surrealistic flights, spins and jumps are interspersed with deft, but relatively realistic, standard swordplay; close-cutting alternates with long shots that reveal the interactive dynamic between the female fighters. Klein astutely observes how one shot in particular enriches the aesthetic effect of the ingeniously choreographed combatants: "He [choreographer Yuen] radically alters our spatial perception when he positions the camera directly above the fighters, looking down, which has the effect . . . of abstracting their contest into a flat, two-dimensional pattern of light-colored movements against a dark background" (29).

Li's arrival serves as a transition to the film's final episode of surrealistic violence. Bouncing into the fray, Li admonishes Jen, saying that she does not deserve the legendary sword. Jen responds by soaring out of the roofless courtyard and skipping over a pond into a thick stand of trees; whereupon, she runs across the treetops and alights upon a forest of tall, lush bamboo. Li follows the girl into the trees in the hopes of winning her over as his (finally, less rambunctious) pupil. What follows is, in the words of Roger Ebert, "a scene of startling daring and beauty, when two protagonists cling to the tops of tall, swaying trees and swing back and forth during a sword fight" (2000).[7] Standing on bending bamboo, the two carry on a conversation during their hostile confrontation. They jockey for fighting position, exchanging places among the trees by means of lofty gyrations. An overhead shot shows them flying at each with swinging swords. Jen glides across to another tree as Li accompanies her to its neighbor, white robes flapping, like majestic birds among the verdant foliage. A long shot presents them swaying atop their respective trees, clashing when their paths cross; "they swing back and forth towards and away from one another, in a languorous and dreamily melancholic spectacle" (O'Day 2004: 212). The pair descends from their bamboo height, their pale robes set off by the large expanse of green from which they emerge.

Having floated down, Jen takes mincing steps across a green pool of water. As she lands on a rock, Li glides onto it to accost the girl anew. Jen repeats, "What do you want?" Li reiterates his wish, "What I've always wanted. To teach you." Stephen Teo points out that this is a stark and striking reversal of *wuxia* convention which stipulates that the neophyte seek out the teacher and ask to be his disciple. Combined with Jen's lack of moral standards, mentioned earlier, this violation of martial arts protocol leads Teo to argue that the film itself is trying to "derail the heroic tradition" (2005: 202). These anomalies, however, could also be interpreted from the perspective of the centrality of women warriors in surrealistically infused *wuxia*: their interests and conflicts seen as generating tensions and discord within the lived and cinematic traditions, not derailing the heroic tradition so much as questioning its assumptions. Jen holds the sword blade to Li's throat and challenges him; she will be Li's pupil if he can retrieve the Green Destiny from her in three moves. Li instantly seizes it in one motion. But when Jen reneges on her agreement and refuses to kneel before her "master," Li declares that she has no use for the fabulous sword and hurls it downstream from the green pond. Jen flies after the sword she covets. We see the steel going under water, followed by Jen who swims after it. Li floats in air after the girl, arms and robe outstretched. He sees a dark, vulture-like figure fly over the water and pluck up Jen and the Green Destiny. It is her tutor, Jade Fox, who disappears with the girl into the windblown, bamboo grove.

Upon finding Jen drugged by Jade, Li and Shu must themselves soon deal with the fiendish former governess. Jade's poison needles eventually kill both her and Li, as Li is not completely successful in parrying them with his sword. Jen rides off to bring back the poison's antidote, but is too late to save Li. Shu gently tells Jen to go to Wudan Mountain where Lo awaits her and implores the girl to be true to herself. Jen appears to be distraught and confused, but goes to the mountain where she and Lo make love during the night. In the morning, Lo goes looking for her and finds her standing on a balcony overlooking a valley. She reminds Lo of the legend he had told her in the desert in which an individual leapt from a mountain and did not die, but had his wishes granted. Jen says, "A faithful heart makes wishes true;" Lo's wish is to be back in the desert with Jen. She dives off the balcony and descends into the mist. A low-angle shot of Jen coming down through the clouds shifts to an overhead view of her with arms spread and gray robe fanned out.

Why can't Jen marry Lo and be legitimated with the *imprimatur* of the formal training of Wudan that Li urges – a resolution to satisfy the Western craving for happy endings? Perhaps she would still be unacceptable to her parents as she seems to have gone through with the original marriage ceremony. Perhaps marrying even Lo, who clearly loves her, would keep Jen from the equality that she finds essential to her fulfillment. She has already rejected Jade and Li as teachers and is not ready for the stolid sisterhood Shu offers. In any event, the quasi-mythic ending leaves us to conjecture that for whatever reason, Jen believes that nothing short of a supernatural force can bring her happiness. The social and political conditions that constrain her provide no options that seem to the rebellious girl likely to realize her ambitions. Jen can find no place on earth, no life that would be worthwhile.

The inability of Jen to harmonize power and love, a recurrent theme in many films in which women warriors are the dominant figure, contrasts interestingly with the way another action heroine succeeds in resolving this persistent tension. The eponymous heroine of the film *Wing Chun* (Yuen Woo Ping, 1994) faces the recurring dilemma that arises for strong women in movies. Learning kung fu and dressing like a man seems to be incompatible with femininity and marriageability. Wendy Arons explains the heroine's difficulty: "As a strong, independent, and decidedly masculinized woman, she poses a threat to men, and has had to resign herself to what she believes is her fate – a life without love and marriage" (2001: 32). As with the Bride and her former cohorts in *Kill Bill*, and now Jen, Wing appears destined to having to choose between two values and the divergent ways of life they support. Yet by the end of her story, Wing is surprisingly able to reclaim her childhood boyfriend without giving up the opportunity to assert herself through mastery of the martial arts. The film's conclusion makes it obvious that "she has not had to compromise her power for love" (Arons 2001: 35).

At least three things can be said about the contrast between the fulfilling end that Wing enjoys and the frustrated, perhaps fanciful, finale that Jen chooses. First, and most obviously, the claim regarding the incompatibility between the female's fighting prowess and domesticity or romantic love is a generalization about action heroines. There can be exceptions. Second, the happy outcome for Wing may be mitigated and somewhat undermined by the fact that her story is presented as a comedy. Unlike the exemplary films on which I focus, a comedy can posit possibilities that dramas cannot as easily get away with: reconciling power and love for the Bride or Jen might very well seem jarring, out of sync with the (non-comedic) narrative trajectory and tone of what has come before. And lastly, the combat in *Wing Chun* is not displayed as surrealistic violence. The generalization about the difficulty of women warriors combining the excitement of martial arts mayhem with the gentler joys of companionable love or motherhood may apply most strongly to those films in which surrealistic spectacle works its transformative magic on interpersonal violence.

The way in which surrealistic film-making transforms familiar masculine action and martial arts cinema may lend itself to privileging women, including how their aspirations strain against social (and cinematic) constraints. Replacing earth with air as the medium of combat seems to symbolize the plight and desire of women. The impossible, surrealistic flight of the female warrior can be viewed as a flight of fancy, a yearning for life on a higher plane. Breaking free of the force of gravity becomes a metaphor for striving for freedom from the numerous, onerous strongholds of patriarchy. Once airborne, the female hero is the equal of any man, but on her own terms: beauty instead of bloodshed, grace instead of gore. But until the reality of their lives changes radically, the exhilarating freedom of movement enjoyed in surrealistically portrayed violence will be but a momentary glimpse of the ideal. Until then, women will either accept a diminished place in a brutally violent world, or, like Jen, throw herself into a mystical dream.

Notes

1 Stephen Teo notes that the proper rendering of the Chinese is "Wudang" (2000).
2 Stephen Teo helpfully points out that in the accurate translation of the Chinese, Jen is named "Jade Dragon" and Lo's name is "Little Tiger." This translation, then, identifies Lo as the "crouching tiger" and Jen as the "hidden dragon" of the film's title (2000).

3 A Mcguffin is an object inserted into the story to help move it along, construed by Hitchcock as a device or gimmick. Sometimes it is not really important, and its lack of importance can add an air of fancy or caprice to the tale
4 Cavell notes that four of his seven film comedies of remarriage include a wooded locale, referred to as "Connecticut;" it is the almost mythic place where lovers discover important truths about one another. He writes, "The exposition of the drama takes place, roughly, in the town, and is both complicated and settled in a shift to the countryside" (p. 120).
5 See Chapter 2 for an extended discussion of the absence or impossibility of romantic fulfillment for the warrior woman.
6 A further reason to take Teo's criticism of the film with a grain of salt is his stringent conception of *wuxia* heroic nature and action. He claims that no *wuxia* movies, save for a pair of King Hu films, really measures up to the (or his) standards of heroism (2000).
7 Ebert explains that in a conversation with him, Ang Lee attested to the fact that the scene involved neither digitization nor stunt people, but was performed by the actors themselves (2000). Stephen Teo interprets the fight between Li and Jen in the bamboo grove as a tribute to the bamboo forest sequence in King Hu's *Touch of Zen*, discussed in some detail in Chapter 1.

Bibliography

Arons, Wendy (2001). "'If Her Stunning Beauty Doesn't Bring You to Your Knees, Her Deadly Drop Kick Will': Violent Women in the Hong Kong Kung Fu Film." *Reel Knockouts: Violent Women in the Movies*, Eds. M. McCaughey and N. King, pp. 27–51. Austin, TX: University of Texas Press.
Bradshaw, Peter (2001). "*Crouching Tiger, Hidden Dragon.*" *The Guardian*, Jan., 2001. www.theguardian.com/film/2001/jan/05/1.
Cavell, Stanley (1981). *Pursuits of Happiness: The Hollywood Comedy of Remarriage*. Cambridge, MA: Harvard University Press.
Ebert, Roger (2000). "*Crouching Tiger, Hidden Dragon.*" Dec., 2000. www.rogerebert.com/reviews/crouching-tiger-hidden-dragon-2000.
Kim, L.S. (2006). "*Crouching Tiger, Hidden Dragon*: Making Women Warriors: A Transnational Reading of Asian Female Action Heroes." *Jump Cut: A Review of Contemporary Media*, 48. www.ejumpcut.org/Archive/Jc48.2006/WomenWarriors.
Klein, Christina (2004). "*Crouching Tiger, Hidden Dragon*: A Diasporic Reading." *Cinema Journal*, 43 (4), Summer, 18–42.
O'Day, Mark (2004). "Beauty in Motion: Gender, Spectacle and Action Babe Cinema." *Action and Adventure Cinema*, Ed. Yvonne Tasker, pp. 201–18. London: Routledge.
Teo, Stephen (2000). "Love and Swords: The Dialectics of Martial Arts Romance: A Review of *Crouching Tiger, Hidden Dragon.*" *Senses of Cinema*. SensesofCinema.com/2000/current-releases-11/crouching.
——— (2005). "*Wuxia* Redux: *Crouching Tiger, Hidden Dragon* as a Model of Late Transnational Production." *Hong Kong Connections: Transnational Imagination in Action Cinema*, Eds. M. Morris, S. Leung Li, and S. Ching-kiu, pp. 191–204. Durham, NC: Duke University Press.

Filmography

Cameron, James (1990). *Terminator 2: Judgment Day*. U.S.
Hu, King (1971). *Touch of Zen*. H.K.
Lee, Ang (2000). *Crouching Tiger, Hidden Dragon*. U.S., H.K., China.
Scott, Ridley (1979). *Alien*. U.S.
——— (1997). *G.I. Jane*. U.S.
Tarantino, Quentin (2003). *Kill Bill (Volume I)*. U.S.
——— (2004). *Kill Bill (Volume II)*. U.S.
Yimou, Zhang (2004). *House of Flying Daggers*. H.K. and China.
Yuen, Woo-Ping (1994). *Wing Chun*. H.K.

5 Surrealistic violence

Women warriors unite

A band of women

The conflicts between women warriors that do much to animate the stories of the previous two films completely vanish in *House of Flying Daggers* (Zhang Yimou, 2004), replaced by unalloyed sisterhood and camaraderie. For example, friendships between women fighters in *Crouching Tiger, Hidden Dragon* (Ang Lee, 2000) are complicated and troubled by power struggles, real and perceived, and divergence in purposes and trust. Jen is unable to commit to the conventions of chivalry or marriage that Shu endorses and twice fights the older woman with considerable animus; and Jen both deceives and is betrayed by her erstwhile governess – *wuxia* master Jade Fox. In both installments of *Kill Bill* (Quentin Tarantino, 2003, 2004), the Bride (aka "Beatrix Kiddo") engages in pitched battle with three female killers who in happier days had been in league with her as fellow assassins for Bill. The Bride directly kills two of these women (bookending the two films) and a third dies after being disabled by the vengeful hero. The Bride also fights with another woman warrior, achieving a non-fatal standoff. In these films, potential and prior friendships between female fighters devolve into emotional and physical conflict.

Unlike both *Crouching Tiger, Hidden Dragon* and *Kill Bill*, there is neither discord nor combat between women in *House of Flying Daggers*, a salient fact that reinforces the bond among the female martial arts experts in this movie. Besides portraying strengthened, univocal relationships among women, the film also develops elements found in *Crouching Tiger, Hidden Dragon*. First, nature figures more dramatically as context and trope rather than merely as an occasional backdrop. Motifs such as flowers and birds accentuate the break with the graphic effusions found in excessive and hyper-violence while calling attention to the cultural connection between the natural and the female. The natural settings, such as different types of forest and fields, are so salient that they arrest attention and function almost like characters in the film-story.

Second, weapons and clothing are more than auxiliaries to the action; they are energetically inscribed in the surrealistic imagery. This extends the visual impact of both the violence (through weaponry) and human form (through attire). Finally, the failed or frustrated romantic ventures of the earlier films are here supplemented with mortal rivalry between the two main male characters for the love of the protagonist. As their protracted battle at film's end is the only fighting in which significant blood is shed, it stands out from the *wuxia* dominated by women warriors. The glaring contrast between the masculine duel of the film's finale and the preceding combat between men and women supports my conclusion that there is a strong kinship between surrealistic violence and its dearth of standard gore with female fighters.

The eponymously named Flying Daggers is an underground organization of women opposed to the corrupt government – significantly, run by men. As far as we can tell, only two men have been part of the cabal: the deceased former leader and a current mole in the army. Women and their distinctive mode of violence are pitted against the male regime with its long-established forms of power and oppression. Masquerading as the blind daughter of the recently slain (male) leader of the organization, Mei (Zhang Ziyi, again) dances at the Peony Pavilion. She begins by performing for Jin (Takeshi Kaneshiro), a government soldier. Pretending to be drunk, Jin grabs Mei and wrestles her to the floor in what appears to be a sexual assault. A captain in the army, Leo (Andy Lau), enters and has Jin arrested, a ploy to thread Jin later into the fabric of the Flying Daggers as a sympathetic outsider. In order to avoid being arrested herself, Mei must exhibit her talent by performing the Echo Game for Leo. We later learn that Leo is himself working for the rebellious organization by going undercover, as a government officer.

Mei must unfurl the preposterously elongated sleeves of her kimono to strike vertically posted drums in the same pattern as the beans that Leo flicks at them. The bean-tossing and the dancer's gracefully executed acrobatics provide a non-violent surrealistic prelude to the film's first display of surrealistic battle. Desson Thomson calls attention to the visual pull of something that might at first seem insignificant: "The slow-motion trajectory of a small bean, hurled from a policeman's hand, is a spectacular thing. It's a stunning, moving image, like a hummingbird caught in action" (2004: 39). Discussing another film, *The Big Heat* (Johnnie To and Andrew Kam, 1988), David Bordwell cites a similar moment in which variations in camera speed emphasize the importance of a physically small object, a tiny cross, to make the general observation: "Hong Kong cinema gives the smallest objects and gestures a kinetic thrust" (2000: 235). Mei proceeds to hit one, then two, then four drums with her silken appendages. After each successful echo the young woman strikes a statuesque pose. Creating a rhythm with an elegant pause may be descended from, or paying homage to, an influential cultural tradition. Discussing the debt of *wuxia* cinema to Peking Opera, David Bordwell writes, "They [opera dancers] punctuate their movements with moments of pure stasis, the technique of *liang hsiang* ('displaying')" (224). The scene is constructed as a staged event within the narrative against the backdrop of the brightly decorated hall, arrayed in candy-colored patterns reminiscent of Dorothy's arrival in the Land of Oz.

Finally, the policeman tosses the entire plate of beans, setting Mei a daunting task. We watch them fly through the air in slow-motion, around the girl like flower petals. The elegant dancer duplicates the percussive pinging of the beans: leaping across the floor in cartwheels, sleeves unfurling like banners. As she spins, jumps and flies, she strikes the fixed drums with a crescendo of sleeve blows. The swirling and twirling of Mei's billowing sleeves suggest the diaphanous wings of a magnificent bird. The camera picks up the pace against the accompanying drumbeat of the assembled musicians: choreography kinetically amplified by cinematography. So far, we have surrealistic movement without violence; however the competition between Leo and Mei and the force with which Mei strikes the drums create an undertone of strife. The balletic-acrobatic prelude morphs into violence when the end of the maiden's kimono preternaturally curls around the sword of the military bean-tosser, like a hand. The transition from dance to combat literally gestures at the entwining of choreography with martial arts – in general and, more pointedly, in the mode of surrealistic violence.

The dancer proceeds to attack Leo, as if the kimono were an elastic arm. The officer hurls flying discs at the young woman which she cuts in two after shifting the confiscated sword to her actual hand. We see shards of the discs fall beautifully, hypnotically to the floor. Instead of cleaving bodies, typical in mega and hyper-violence, we watch these miniature weapons sliced apart. During the ensuing swordplay, Mei is flung backward into the air. She does a back-flip in slow-motion, her gown and sleeves opening like a butterfly. The swordfight resembles a surrealistic *pas de deux*, as the pair float, run on air, flip and rotate in impossible ways. Once we later discover that Leo is a mole in the army for the Flying Daggers, we should be puzzled by the fight between him and Mei. Who is it being staged for? As there is no one around to be taken in by the duel between individuals who are actually comrades, such as Leo's military troops or the duped Jin, we realize in retrospect that the brief but exciting combat makes sense only from the standpoint of the viewer, who does not yet know of the complicity between the two. After the fight, Mei is imprisoned by Leo and this charade is for the sake of Jin.

The subversive Flying Daggers ironically inverts the power relation governing the Peony Pavilion. Within the pavilion, Geisha women are subservient to men, catering to their sensual desires, but as members of the insurgent underground, women warriors dominate. The inversion is visually symbolized by the active role played by Mei's costume. Fashionable clothing of women is typically repressive; it limits female movement and is designed to please the eyes of men. Yet here, Mei's garb functions as an extension and augmentation of her agency in opposition to a man: transformed by surrealistic violence from an accoutrement of passive adornment to an instrument of active self-determination.

As the story unfolds, all the principals are unmasked as pretending to be something or someone they are not. The madam of the Peony Pavilion turns out to be a high-ranking officer in the rebellious organization. She will also pretend to be the new female leader of the Flying Daggers, Nia. And the dashing Jin, who frees Mei from prison as if her new ally, is really the enemy – a police officer, as Leo is supposed to be, and the partner of the dissembling Leo. Kwai-Cheung Lo elaborates on the pervasive assumption of false roles by the main characters: "Every character is engaged in different levels of deceit, and intertwined with trust and betrayal" (2007: 133).

Flight and fight

As in *Crouching Tiger, Hidden Dragon*, the story is propelled by a beautiful young woman who is adept at the martial arts. Mei is at the crux of two deceptive schemes that mirror one another. "Clearly it is Mei, the mysterious character, setting in motion the entire movie: the government follows her to find the rebel's (*sic*) base while the rebels use her as bait to set a trap for the official force" (Lo 2007: 134). The enactment of this barebones plot consists chiefly in Mei and her ersatz defender, Jin, fleeing government troops. This linear movement of the couple is interrupted by surrealistic skirmishes with their assailants, accompanied by intermittent romance and revelations of deception. Although we catch a brief glimpse of the government's army advancing into what may indeed be a trap set by the Flying Daggers at film's end, such a denouement is omitted, leaving us to wonder. The linear plot movement becomes gradually tangled until finally knotted in the conclusion of the film-story by a standard love triangle. "[Mei] is also the elusive object of love and lust for the two male protagonists [Jin and Leo]" (Lo 2007: 134). Mei has long been adored by Leo, who has postponed his amorous designs in the service of the Flying Daggers for several repressed years. But as she pairs with Jin to form a martial arts team, Mei finds herself romantically involved with him, leaving Leo bitter, in the lurch. It is perhaps ironic that only the female object of their romantic ardor dies at the climax of the story, leaving the two male rivals bloodied and bereft, but apparently alive.

The government wants to locate and eliminate the new leader of the Flying Daggers. To achieve this, Leo directs Jin to gain Mei's confidence in the hopes that she will lead him to the headquarters of the rebellious women. Unbeknownst to Jin, of course, Leo's goal is actually to lure the army into an ambush. To effect the plan into which Jin is enlisted, he must spring Mei from imprisonment. Jin disarms a coterie of guards with just his fists and feet to free the purportedly blind dancer, and they ride off on horseback. Jin's ostensible, and spurious, rationale for helping her is that he hates the corrupt government and admires the Flying Daggers. Mei is not supposed to know that Jin is really an army officer aiming to destroy the underground organization.

During their journey through a forest, Jin leaves Mei alone in order to retrieve the dagger pouch she has dropped. Mei fends off a brace of attacking soldiers until finally brought down by four more. Jin has been running back to Mei and returns at this moment (with the missing daggers). He looses four arrows, shown in a trailing shot in slow-motion, wending their way through spaces between the trees. Although shot sequentially, the arrows (impossibly) hit the four belligerents simultaneously, lifting them off their feet. They fly apart, in dance-like synchronization, as if petals parting around the flower-maiden, leaving Mei free in their midst. The fluidity of this sleight-of-timing prompts reviewers such as Roger Ebert to find the photography of the film replete with "elegant ingenuity" (2004). The quartet of apparently slain soldiers soon arises unharmed: no bloodshed, no death. Not only are the arrows not realistically lethal, but their progress toward their targets proceeds in aesthetically riveting fashion.

Jin leads his companion to fresh horses, builds a fire and creates a bathing pool by spreading apart some water lilies in a nearby pond. Jin and Mei first discuss the Flying Daggers and soon lie on the ground, kissing passionately. When Mei stops further amorous play, Jin gets up, a bit frustrated. They talk about ardor and Mei asks whether a playboy like Jin is ever "for real." The bath and respite from violence echo the desert bath of Jen and her subsequent sojourn with the charming outlaw Lo in *Crouching Tiger, Hidden Dragon*. Both settings create narrative space for the woman warrior to let down her guard and yield to romantic inclination. The two loci of passion represent an escape from the perils of violence as well as the conventions of everyday life: the aristocratic norms in *Crouching Tiger, Hidden Dragon*, and the military code in *House of Flying Daggers*. Neither heroine is married to her lover and each is the equal of her romantic male partner. What is also telling about these scenes of sexual intimacy is the way they further distinguish the surrealistic action heroine from muscular male and female protagonists.

As mentioned in earlier chapters, the surrealistic heroine is unlike the Bride or Lara Croft; she does not display bulging biceps, in fact hardly exhibits her body as it is almost always clothed. Reinforcing her dissimilarity from the muscular champions is the surrealistic heroine's capacity for romance and sex with her love interest. Yvonne Tasker finds further continuity between the two genders of powerfully built action hero in that both avoid sex or are unable to accommodate it to their life of violence: "Like the male hero, it seems that the action heroine cannot be in control of an adult sexuality" (1993: 138). The romantic, sexual activity of the surrealistic heroine is all the more ironic since, be-robed, she is not sexualized the way such masculinized (but scantily clad) female heroes as Barb Wire or Salt is.

The surrealistic heroine's romantic sexuality is suggestive, especially when viewed in conjunction with the stifling social conditions, the motif of nature, and the absence of brutality. It might imply that the aims and meaning of surrealistic violence are quite different from the import of such alternate modes of violence as realistic or hyper-violence. Although the muscular action heroine is partially liberated by being at the heart of her film-story and its action, she is still bound by the cinematic (and perhaps social) conventions that govern the Schwarzeneggers and Van Dammes. She is not free to enjoy or be much interested in heterosexual intimacy. As the dominant persona in surrealistic violence, however, the new action heroine can be construed as struggling to become truly liberated from these cinematic and social limitations. She is capable of and aspires to a complete life, one that includes fulfilling intimacy in the private sphere as well as exhilarating combat in the socio-political realm. Her independence of the laws of gravity may indicate the quest for freedom from the social norms that weigh her down. But until the socio-political liberation is achieved, freedom in private intimacy for the surrealistic heroine can only be furtive and sporadic.

While Mei sleeps, Jin has a rendezvous with Leo in the woods. Jin says that he has gained no information about the Flying Daggers. Foreshadowing the embroiled love triangle that is forming, Leo warns Jin not to fall for Mei. We later learn that Leo has loved Mei since before he went undercover as an officer in the government's army.

In the next scene of surrealistically shaped violence, Mei once more grapples with a brace of soldiers. The cinematography and editing of the action subtly structure the conflict to further its poetic effect. Mei flings one of her daggers backhanded and the camera tracks it turning horizontally, in slow-motion, through the air before hitting a soldier in the throat. As a result, a second soldier moves more cautiously behind his shield. This time with a forehand thrust, Mei lets go a second dagger; it miraculously curves around the shield, slitting this soldier's throat as well. The pause that ensues exemplifies one of the ways in which editing can "enhance the tempo of the combat" for David Bordwell: "a cut to a static shot can interrupt a burst of action, providing a caesura" (2000: 237). The break in action serves to accentuate the preceding and succeeding violence. The pause is momentary, however, as four more soldiers advance on Mei. She runs over the second and third, spinning 360 degrees in mid-air, clanking her sword against shield and sword upon her descent. Shot from above, we watch her cartwheel upward into the air as the soldiers below separate. Again, Bordwell's film-making observations are apt, as the editing creates "a syncopated rhythm" by intercutting "slow motion and normal motion" (237). Though barely discernible as it occurs, such rhythms supplement the enthralling surrealistic movement with a harmonic undertone, like a resonant musical chord or linguistic connotation.

Jin is clearly perplexed and upset by the attack as Leo had assured him that there would be no more fighting. He hurries to Mei's rescue, dashing about, letting four arrows fly. The camera follows three of the arrows in slow-motion, as if they were birds in flight, until their targets are downed. The last arrow, viewed from behind, parts a meadow of tall wild flowers before glancing off the fourth soldier's shield. It appears to resume in a new trajectory that comes to rest in his exposed side. This time the pursuers do seem to be slain, but only a trace of blood shows up on a sword.

Surrealistic weaponry

Rendering airborne knives and arrows in slow-motion adds the grace of turning, skimming, weaving weaponry to the aesthetic of the physical movement of the combatants, whose acrobatic displays are typically shot in real time. The slowed movement of weapons in surrealistically depicted violence does not detract from the aesthetic effect as it might in other, more graphic or intensely violent cinema. Speaking of such cinema, Geoff King argues, "Bullets and other weapons can be slowed down, but to do so more than fleetingly is to risk losing the vital element of pace" (2014: 102). Slowing down the trajectory of bullets and the like would weaken their effect because they are in the service of an aggressive aesthetic. King identifies the purpose of such action films as promoting an "impact aesthetics," one that includes rapid motion toward the viewer (98–99). The aesthetic aim of surrealistic *wuxia* films, however, is the opposite of an aesthetic in which "aggressive movements assault the viewer head on" (101). Rather, the languorous pace of slowed weaponry dovetails with the surrealistic violence of flowing robes, and somersaulting, spinning or floating bodies to create a dreamscape in which violence is transfigured into a spectacle at a distance, one that does not confront or threaten the viewer.

In the now sun-drenched plain, the couple clasp hands and begin to flee. They are soon surrounded by another cadre of soldiers. The pair clash with their antagonists, run a few paces, so in tempo with the movement of the soldiers that they remain encircled. The green of the soldiers' uniforms vibrates to the silver of their eight swords, raised in unison. The soldiers always seem to attack in even multiples: two, four, and now forming an encasing octet. But flying daggers pierce the necks of four of the soldiers and the nimble pair takes care of the remaining foursome. Peter Bradshaw characterizes the captivating camera-work as presenting a "daggers-eye view" (2004: 2). While this is somewhat accurate, most of the shots include the daggers themselves and so cannot quite be from their "point of view."

Although *House of Flying Daggers* makes greater surrealistic use of weaponry than *Crouching Tiger, Hidden Dragon*, an earlier film by the director of the former is yet more ingenious in photographing weapons in aesthetically dramatic fashion. In his film *Hero* (2002), Zhang Yimou aestheticizes weaponry by synthesizing it with nature – another dramatic element that *House of Flying Daggers* also celebrates. During an early fight in the rain, an enemy of the hero rapidly twirls his sword and water droplets fly off, in a wondrous whorl, like a galaxy of stars. The hero flies through the screen of water and stabs his opponent who seems surprised, as if the hero had penetrated a protective shield. Later in the film, leaves play a similar role, being integrated into the combat. This time, it is a conflict involving two women: the women dive, spring and leap through gorgeous, autumnal, blowing leaves. At one point, their fighting looks like a duet of balletic spinning through the air, with one of the adversaries rotating horizontally through swirling leaves, toward her opponent. Once the skirmish is over, leaves fall, their color deepening to a rich, blood red that corresponds to the same intense hue as the surrounding trees.

Perhaps most impressive is what seems to be an imaginary battle between Hero and a martial arts expert named "Sword" that takes place above a lake. Reflections in the water picturesquely double their springing, spinning and gliding above the surface of the lake. When their swords dip into the water, the movement is reminiscent of Sword's calligraphic brush strokes earlier in the film-story, thereby creating an imagined doubling in the memory that reinforces the visual duplication created by the water on the screen. In a much earlier film, *Eastern Condors* (1987), director Sammo Hung goes one better by actually transforming unlikely nature into weaponry by means of slow-motion. Hardly a natural object well-suited to be weaponized, such as bamboo shaped into spears, an apparently innocuous swath of broadleaf becomes deadly when thrown in slow-motion.

Show-stopping spectacle

After their escape from the soldiers, Mei drapes herself over the back of Jin as they sit in the field. This time, Mei initiates intimacy. Convinced by their joint struggle of Jin's sincerity, she caresses Jin's face and kisses him. Further reversing their first romantic embrace, Jin now breaks off the lovemaking. Miffed by his balking, Mei tells Jin to leave and not to worry about her. Jin refuses to leave her, but meets again with Leo in the forest. He reminds Leo that that they had agreed to halt the attacks by the soldiers. Leo replies that the general sent the soldiers and they do not know who Jin is. The original scheme hatched by the Flying Daggers is spiraling out of control as the general is taking over; he hopes to draw the Flying Daggers into the open by attacking Jin and Mei. During another conversation about their relationship, Mei reiterates her theme, asking Jin, "Are you for real?" Jin responds that she should not take things so seriously and reprises his self-description as the "wind," always moving (echoing Jen's simplistic conception of freedom in *Crouching Tiger, Hidden Dragon*). At Jin's unwillingness to commit to her, Mei thanks him for all he has done and rides off.

What follows is a prolonged battle in a bamboo forest that spectacularly rounds out the film's portrayal of surrealistic violence. Were the film a Broadway musical, it would arguably be the show-stopper. The forest itself is not merely a setting for the surrealistic combat, but is intertwined, in color and movement, with the actions of the antagonists. As Roger Ebert notes, the bamboo grove "functions like a kinetic art installation" (2004). Once again alone, Mei ducks down in a sea of green bamboo and gray mist, leaves fall and trees sway in a low-angle shot. The young woman rises to her feet, sensing trouble. Male soldiers swarm down in silhouette from trees and vines, spears drawn, only to be kicked aside by Mei. The besieged heroine prepares for the assault by bracing herself between two trees in a 180-degree leg-split, bamboo pole at the ready. She parries sharpened bamboo spears that are hurled at her; a rear-view trailing shot follows their flight toward the solitary female fighter. We see several spears deflected, splitting trunks of bamboo trees. The scene is drenched in hues and shades of green, including the ringed bamboo of trees and spears, leaves, and the uniforms of the soldiers. The morning mist augments the dream-like quality of the surrealism of the violence.

A pair of assailants descends head first from above but are quickly dispatched by Mei when they arrive. The measured downward movement carries a predatory menace even though less flamboyantly surrealistic than purely aerial descent or fantastic horizontal scampering across the woodland heights. As more adversaries slide down tree trunks, Mei readies herself on the forest floor and succeeds in knocking a couple away. However, she is soon surrounded, beating off a clutch of sword-brandishing soldiers with nothing but a bamboo pole which begins to split and fray at its end. Finally, the pole is shattered. Mei scurries, defending herself on the run. Just as Mei is trapped, Jin bounds once more into the fray. The couple flees with soldiers in close pursuit.

Jin slashes trees with his broad sword, whose collapse temporarily slows the soldiers' advance. From ground level, we watch the belligerents climb trees and then fabulously swim, run and whirligig in the air from treetop to treetop. Air and ground provide parallel planes of chase. As the antagonists dog the couple, they throw spears, horizontally repositioning the naturally upright stands of bamboo. Below, Mei and Jin hurry through a mist-cloaked, dense stand of trees as flying spears punctuate their footfalls on the forest floor. A. O. Scott astutely observes how both visual and auditory symmetries contribute to the power of the extended sequence: "The bamboo-forest scene is not just a bravura exercise in vertical and horizontal choreography, as fighters swoop down from the leafy canopy and scurry across the ground. It is also a heroic feat of sound design, with the whistle of the bamboo fronds played in counterpoint to the impact of cudgels and spears" (2004). We hear the spears hurtle through the air with bass-like groans, complementing the high-pitched chanting on the soundtrack. The lower register seems to be the motif of the villains while the upper notes signal the champions, thereby reversing in pitch their physical locations aloft and aground.

The soldiers finally spring a trap of pointed bamboo stakes that snap up from the forest floor. Cut off from escape, the couple is surrounded by men perched in the trees, spears poised, mimicking avian beaks and claws. The spears come clanking down, creating a perfectly constructed cage. Peter Bradshaw remarks on this inventive deployment of bamboo in the film-story: "Bamboo canes are chopped down with stroboscopic brilliance to form palisade-cages and improvised spears" (2004: 2). Resigned to defeat, the couple talk. Mei tells Jin that he should not have come back, to which he replies, "I came back for you." The soldiers on the ground close in. Mei reaches out and clasps Jin's hand in her own. From nowhere, dozens of the miraculous knives zoom into view. They simultaneously sink into the backs of the assailants; as earlier in the film, soldiers fly backward like petals disclosing a blossom in the heart of an enclosed flower. More knives send the other troops crashing down from their lofty posts in the trees. Mei exclaims, "Nia," referring to the new female leader of the Flying Daggers.

As an army of green clad women emerges, the leader releases a final dagger which weaves its way toward the caged couple, whereupon it wondrously dismantles the enclosing bamboo spears. Once again, women dominate: first as the focal point of the action, then as erstwhile knights in shining armor. Reversing the standard narrative of male heroes rescuing damsels in distress, women now rescue beleaguered women, and save a man in the bargain.

The vibrant sequence in the bamboo forest effectively ends the surrealistic fighting in the film. What follows plays out and brings to a consummation the tensions in the love triangle that had been tightening since Jin initially fled with Mei. Peter Bradshaw describes it succinctly: "The triangulated relationship is a fraught drama of double-cross and triple cross" (2004: 2). The fact that the audience shares in the surprise at some of the revelations adds bite to what could have been a somewhat hackneyed story-line. Jin chats amicably about Mei and marriage with the erstwhile madam of the Peony Pavilion, who is now pretending to be Nia, but he is soon bound in a net and tied up. When he asks what is going on, Leo is brought in, similarly bound, and Nia's double explains that the government was trying to catch her by following Mei (whom they had been tricked into thinking was the blind daughter of the former leader of the Flying Daggers).

Love's labor and loss

When Mei enters, Jin, along with viewers, is astonished to discover that she is not blind and therefore not the daughter of the former leader. He remarks, "It's all been an act," implying also a reference to Mei's putative feelings for him as well. Here the film interrogates the psychological implications of behavioral subterfuge by commenting on the unanticipated nexus between outer role-playing (such as disguising oneself as a soldier, as Leo does) and one's inner emotional life.[1] Recall Mei's repeated questioning of whether Jin was "for real," probing to learn whether he truly cared for her. Each of the characters in the love triangle soon discovers that outer pretense can alter inner reality.

Nia's surrogate, her lieutenant, takes Leo out to the forest. Leo's declaration that she is not Nia is likely to surprise members of the audience since we have no reason to suspect this additional imposture: first Mei and now the madam of the Peony Pavilion, as central female characters double the duplicity of the main male characters. The lieutenant cuts Leo free of his bondage, telling him that he has done a good job as a spy planted in the military (by the Flying Daggers). She notes that he and Mei, at Nia's own instigation, have "successfully set up a trap for the general." When Leo complains that he still loves Mei, has not seen her for three years, and has had to watch her flirt with another man, the lieutenant relents, and permits him to see Mei.

Mei joins Leo and reprises a reversed version of their Echo Game at the Peony Pavilion by flinging a pebble through the air. The camera tracks the pebble in slow-motion and Leo, blindfolded (even as Mei had posed as sightless), releases a dagger that splits the pebble as it lands on the trunk of a bamboo tree. Mei smiles and tosses another pebble which ricochets off one tree before plonking into another. Leo hits both spots with simultaneously flung knives, and removes his blindfold. After Mei tells Leo that she knows he would do anything for her, Leo nuzzles and holds her. He kisses her and lowers her to the forest floor. Mei seems to enjoy Leo's caresses, but turns aside his attempt to kiss her lips. When Leo asks, "Do you love him?" Mei looks at him without answering. Mei cries as Leo notes that it was only "an act between you and him," and points out that she and Jin have no future. Leo resumes kissing and becomes forceful when Mei rebuffs him again. She gasps and struggles.

A following shot shows a thrown dagger striking Leo in the shoulder, from behind. The real Nia appears alongside her trusted assistant, but with face hidden by the standard broad-brimmed, conical green hat worn by the women. Nia says, "You can't force a woman against her will." Leo laments, "I have sacrificed three years for you. How could you love Jin in just three days?" Ah, the wonder of love's mysterious alchemy. Nia instructs Mei to kill Jin who is, after all, a government soldier sent to ferret out Nia and her stronghold.

Mei leads the blindfolded, bound Jin, but this time in a different forest. Instead of the enveloping green of the bamboo copse she shared with Leo, Mei is now accompanying Jin in a wooded glade of green and yellow leaves, amidst silver-trunked trees which have carpeted the ground with bright orange leaves pierced by shafts of sunlight. Two men, two forests. Mei and Jin pass through the woods into a field framed by hills similarly adorned with leaves turning from green to yellow and orange. The colorful venue of the forest and hills, in contrast with the familiar green of the former bamboo grove, suggests how the vibrancy of Jin has captivated Mei, eclipsing the worthy but staid loyalty of the familiar Leo. Mei tells Jin that she left him earlier to save his life, "but you still followed me." In one smooth, upward stroke of her sword, Mei cuts Jin free of his ropes. Instead of executing the deceitful, government soldier, Mei makes passionate love with him.

They lie on their backs and Mei tells Jin to leave. He asks Mei to come with him, but Mei is conflicted. Although she loves Jin, she is indebted to Leo for saving her life many times. Before they part, Jin repeats his proposal, prompting the pair to revisit their wistful conversation about roaming around, free as the wind. Jin rides away, but Mei soon rides after him. Galloping across a field, Mei is knocked from her horse by a dagger thrown by Leo that lodges above her heart. Mei gets up, bleeding from the mouth and chest. Leo blames Mei for "forcing" him to kill her. Mei collapses on the ground having told Leo that she knew he would do this.

In the meantime, Jin has turned around and hurried back for Mei. After he dismounts, Jin is attacked by Leo. In the midst of their swordfight, the two men bark out recriminations at each other with regard to Mei. The combat is good, but surrealistic flight and acrobatics is diminished by the anger-fueled, bloody contest. The camera makes a quick-cut to a separate scene of government troops advancing, with swords brandished, in a bamboo forest. They appear to be closing in on a hut, perhaps part of Nia's scheme to ambush them. But we never find out, as the larger conflict between the Flying Daggers and the government forces is abandoned altogether in favor of the resolution of the violent rivalry for Mei.

As Jin and Leo fight on, a mounting snowfall begins to blanket the ground, covering them and the fallen Mei. The rivals slash and cut one another, scuffle and tumble in the snow, and pummel one another with their fists. Gone is all the graceful elegance of surrealistic violence. Instead, we see passion-driven brutality: as they slash at each other, blood flies into the air in small spurts against a background of densely falling white flakes. Bright blood also flecks the clean white snow on the ground.[2] Back to back, the men simultaneously plunge their swords into each other. Both are staggered. The snow-drenched scene is visually stunning, despite the fact that more blood is shed in it than in the rest of the film combined. It is as though combat exclusively between men, and over a woman, has its barbarity bared because shorn of the mitigating female influence that informs the rarefied beauty of surrealistic violence. Moreover, could autumn turn so quickly into a fierce, wintry snow storm? The onslaught, escalation and accumulation of the snowfall seems to protract the battle as if it lasts for days or weeks rather than hours: seasonal time stretched to suggest the timelessness of love's triangulation.

Mei gets up and tells Leo to let Jin go. Jin urges Mei to leave the dagger in place as it is staunching the flow of her blood. Jin throws down his sword and hobbles toward Mei to keep her from removing the dagger that Leo had jealously hurled. The scene is now virtually all white. Leo pretends to flick his remaining dagger, prompting Mei to pull hers out and toss it in order to intercept the anticipated flight of Leo's knife toward Jin. Instead, Mei's dagger splits a drop of blood that left Leo's hand when he feigned the knife toss. Mei smiles at both men. Jin is aghast because Mei has sealed her death by removing the embedded dagger and hurries, limping through the snow to hold her. Leo, who had been standing like a statue holding the unthrown dagger outstretched in his hand, lowers his arm and drops the blade in the snow. He trudges off into the snowy woods. The two soldiers had been fighting to the death over Mei, but she is the one who perishes, and they appear to survive.

On first blush, it might seem as though the brutal battle between Jin and Leo subverts the contra-violent aura that the film's surrealism had so carefully cast over the preceding physical confrontations. After all the blood-less aerial acrobatics and serpentine knife-throwing we have been enjoying, the story concludes with two men fighting it out on the solid ground, without recourse to breathtaking somersaults, impossible leaps, or evasive spins. Instead, we watch an old-fashioned slugfest, in which gouging, bashing and stabbing render both combatants bloody and perhaps mortally battered. Of all the violence in the film, this one is singular: it alone excludes women and it alone is driven by passion and romantic competition. These glaring exceptions to the major motifs and tropes of the movie separate its conclu-sion from the rest of the film, thereby insulating the surrealistic violence that characterizes the previous fighting from the atypical blood and gore of its finale. So far from undermining or tainting the harmony between the transformative nature of surrealistic violence and women warriors, the grue-some clash between the men who vie for Mei symbolically and ironically reinforces it.

Women and surrealistic violence

This leads me to wonder whether there is a significant connection between surrealistically designed violence and woman as cinematic warrior. To claim that there is a necessary link between the two would be an over-statement. Since the surrealism is found in purely formal dimensions of film-making, it cannot exclude men as protagonists. And there are plenty of movies that celebrate surrealistic violence but have men as the action heroes. Yet, given the prevalence of male-dominated action films, cou-pling women with violence that markedly departs from the former sug-gests something deeper than a matter of novelty or expedience. There might be more than a merely passing, contingent connection between surrealistic movie combat and the centrality of women: their form, con-flicts and interests. There might be a tie weaker than logical necessity but stronger than just happenstance, something like a natural or inherent affinity. The connection could be analogous to the natural fit, for example, between music and dance or male physiology and football (versus, say, women's bodies and the balance beam). Other examples include the way mathematical ability fuels mastery in chess and music or the way certain colors lend themselves to the expression of mood.

As with *Crouching Tiger, Hidden Dragon*, the surrealistic violence that animates *House of Flying Daggers* celebrates the female form, costumed and aligned with nature, as women manage to carve out space for romantic passion in the midst of a battle-filled life. Even weapons move magically under the spell of female-centered conflict. In both films, the female hero wages war against repressive social norms as much as against her particular adversaries, because her aspirations, including her zest for martial arts, are blocked by society's traditions and arrangements of power. The fabulous, surrealistic violence that is so well-suited to the agility and strengths of the female warrior can be understood as crystallizing the struggle of women in general. Freedom from the pull of gravity suggests the freedom from the mundane but formidable forces that keep women from complete and satisfying lives. Our two *wuxia* films of surrealistic violence imply that for women to prevail, violence as we typically know and experience it will have to be transformed into martial dance: an imitation or representation of martial combat that transcends its grisly history in both the real and cinematic world. When women take over, their resonance with nature, life and romantic love will finally displace male-centered warfare.

Surrealistic violence is positioned as anti-violence, a repudiation of the devastation and suffering wrought by most cinematic and real life mayhem. Moreover, women are usually the victims of male violence, whether on the movie screen or the street. It therefore seems fitting that the heroes of surrealistic violence be women. Both sides of the violent equation are transformed in the process. The surrealistic champions offer neither bristling biceps nor chiseled thighs and their opponents rarely bleed, lose limbs or die. The audience witnesses violence without its typical natural or cinematic effects. It has become something else, feminized by beauty and grace. Less realistic than its predecessors, the enchantment cast by surrealistic violence feeds a sense of allegory, aimed at enlightenment as much as entertainment. When transfigured by surrealism, violence becomes ethereal choreography, filled with symbolic promise.

Notes

1 Roger Ebert astutely notes a parallel with the pretense and love triangle in Alfred Hitchcock's *Notorious* (1946), Roger Ebert (2004).
2 The image anticipates Quentin Tarantino's blood-stippled white cotton ball in *Django Unchained* (2012), discussed in Chapters 1 and 3.

Bibliography

Bordwell, David (2000). *Planet Hong Kong: Popular Cinema and the Art of Entertainment*. Cambridge, MA: Harvard University Press.
Bradshaw, Peter (2004). "*House of Flying Daggers*." *The Guardian*, Dec. 24. www.theguardian.com/film/2004/dec/24/2.
Ebert, Roger (2004). "*House of Flying Daggers*." www.rogerebert.com/review/house-of-flying-daggers.
King, Geoff (2014). *Spectacular Narratives: Contemporary Hollywood and Frontier Mythology*. London: I.B. Tauris.

Lo, Kwai-Cheung (2007). "Copies of Copies in Hollywood and Hong Kong Cinema." *Hong Kong Film, Hollywood and the New Global Cinema: No Film Is an Island*, Eds. G. Marchetti and T. See Kamp, pp. 126–36. New York: Routledge.

Scott, A.O. (2004). "Silk Brocade Soaked in Blood and Passion." *New York Times*, Oct. 9. nytimes.com/2004/10/09/movies/silk-brocade-soaked-in-blood-and-passion.

Tasker, Yvonne (1993). *Spectacular Bodies: Gender, Genre and the Action Cinema*. New York and London: Routledge.

Thomson, Desson (2004). "'Daggers' Flies Off the Screen." *Washington Post*, Dec. 17, WE 39.

Filmography

Fleming, Victor (1939). *The Wizard of Oz*. U.S.

Hung, Sammo (1987). *Eastern Condors*. H.K.

Lee, Ang (2000). *Crouching Tiger, Hidden Dragon*. U.S., H.K., China.

Tarantino, Quentin (2003). *Kill Bill (Volume I)*. U.S.

——— (2004). *Kill Bill (Volume II)*. U.S.

——— (2012). *Django Unchained*. U.S.

To, Johnnie and Andrew Kam (1988). *The Big Heat*. H.K.

Yimou, Zhang (2002). *Hero*. H.K.

——— (2004). *House of Flying Daggers*. H.K. and China.

Index